THE
CURSE
OF
BIGNESS

About the author

Tim Wu is Professor of Law, Science and Technology at Columbia Law School and a contributing writer for the *New York Times*. He previously worked for Barack Obama and is the author of *The Master Switch* and *The Attention Merchants*.

THE CURSE OF BIGNESS

How Corporate Giants
Came to Rule the World

TIM WU

Atlantic Books
London

First published in the United States in 2018 by Columbia Global Reports, New York.

Published in hardback in Great Britain in 2020 by Atlantic Books, an imprint of Atlantic Books Ltd.

10 9 8 7 6 5 4 3 2 1

A CIP catalogue record for this book is available from the British Library.

Hardback ISBN: 978 1 83895 082 8
E-book ISBN: 978 1 83895 083 5

Printed in Great Britain by CPI Group (UK) Ltd, Croydon CR0 4YY

Atlantic Books
An imprint of Atlantic Books Ltd
Ormond House
26–27 Boswell Street
London
WC1N 3JZ

www.atlantic-books.co.uk

For Gillian Elizabeth, my mother,
who always thought I should
have been a scientist

CONTENTS

INTRODUCTION

We are three decades into a major global experiment. What happens when the nations of the world weaken their controls on the size and power of industrial giants? What happens when countries, in the name of globalism, grandly subsidize their wealthiest and most powerful firms?

The answers, I think, are clear. Look at the global economy and witness the rule of concentrated monopolies and oligopolies, the by-product of decades of consolidation across industries like agriculture, finance and pharmaceuticals. Witness the power of the great tech platforms, like Google and Facebook, which have gained an extraordinary power over our lives and collectively know more about everyone than anyone. And behold the unconscionable concentration of global wealth, the yawning gap between the rich and poor, most clearly manifest in the international class of billionaires who inhabit their own sovereignty.

Back in the 1990s, the promise of globalization was that the elimination of trade barriers and the rise of global supply chains would yield a broad spreading of wealth to everyone. There was, to be sure, debate over who would benefit from such competition, and worries about displaced workers and environmental impact. But in retrospect, the advocates of globalization – and even some of its critics – forgot something more fundamental about how capitalism works. They failed to realize that globalization might breed a new class of monopoly that would drain wealth from everyone: workers, suppliers and producers. They also forgot that some nations would seek precisely that outcome in the name of progress.

The result is that a great concentration of wealth and private power has now transformed and radicalized politics around the globe, as a disaffected and declining middle class, those who feel left behind, have come to support increasingly radical solutions. In nations around the world – Brazil, Britain, Hungary, the United States and others – have emerged nationalist movements that, in their more extreme forms, resemble the most dangerous movements of the 1930s. They blame the same scapegoats – immigrant workers, foreigners, gays or elite conspiracies – for the diminishment of the middle class, while calling for an enlargement of state power in a manner that can only be described as terrifying.

What we are facing is a global 'Curse of Bigness' that represents a profound and dangerous threat to economic thriving for the broader public, but also to liberal democracy itself. For we have, incautiously, given up on the ideal of economic democracy, while forgetting that economic dictatorship tends to beget political dictatorship. The operating premise of a democracy is that it makes the people of a nation sovereign over their affairs. Yet around the world, in so many nations, people do not feel that way.

The patterns we are seeing should be familiar to any student of twentieth-century history. If we learned one thing from the last century, it should have been this: the road to fascism and dictatorship is paved with failures of economic policy to serve the needs of the broader public. Gross inequality and material suffering feed a dangerous appetite for nationalistic and extremist leadership. Yet, as if blind to these lessons, we are going down the same path.

The questions we need to face are these: Is tolerance of global monopoly and oligopoly actually compatible with the premise of basic equality among citizens, industrial freedom, or democracy itself? Can we create broad-based wealth in many regions, not just a few, and also a real sense of opportunity in economies dominated by monopolists? Is there just too much concentrated private power in too few hands, which has too much influence over government? The questions, I think, answer themselves.

But it is not enough to diagnose the problem. The goal of this book is to rediscover a classic answer to the problem of bigness: a programme of anti-monopoly and the redistribution of monopoly profit. To do this we need to relearn the lessons taught by two groups of important thinkers: the European Ordoliberals and those of the Anglo-American anti-monopoly tradition. These are thinkers whose influence was paramount after the catastrophe of the Second World War.

Unfortunately, over the last thirty years, beginning in the United States, the anti-monopoly tradition has begun to shrink, and in some instances, nearly disappear. The problem is an overindulgence in the extreme ideas first advocated by American conservatives in the 1960s that have been repackaged and globalized. Stated succinctly, an embrace of technocratic neoliberalism has transmuted into the tolerance or even an embrace of monopoly, while shedding the historic concerns over excessive political power and political influence.

The ideas that originated with the American right, and severely weakened the anti-monopoly tradition in its home country, have spread to the centre and around the world. In Europe, the home of the Ordoliberal tradition, competition officials, while superficially very active, have nonetheless too often accepted and approved the consolidation campaigns of global industries. While well intentioned, in the pursuit of technocratic rigour, Europeans have too easily accepted a narrow view of their powers, sensitive only to questions of efficiency and with greater indifference to the growth of private power or the potential corruption of democracy.

Finally, most of the major Asian economies have been too willing to accept close ties between private industry and government, sometimes embracing state-directed capitalism. This variety of capitalism can be very effective over the short term; but its longer historical record is troubling for not just economic but political reasons. Japan, both before and after the Second World War, is the most recent nation to demonstrate both the political and economic dangers, and China has begun to make clear the alarming possibilities that come from the potent mixture of private and public power.

The democratic nations desperately need to do something about concentrated private power and wealth and their effect on politics. It is striking that documents like the Magna Carta, the US Constitution, the Treaty of Lisbon and the UN Charter were written to restrain the exercise of unaccountable public power, yet we have nothing that really does the same for unchecked private power. If we do not act, the alternative is not appealing. The old cliché is that those who fail to learn from history are doomed to repeat it. We have returned to the struggle between democratic and authoritarian systems, and if democracy does not provide some answer to the problems caused by unrestrained capitalism, it may not win.

This book, in structure, is a simple story of there and back again. After detailing our current economic state, it returns to history to focus on the twentieth century's struggle with bigness, and its political consequences, with a focus on Germany and Japan before the Second World War. The book introduces the principles that underlie the anti-monopoly tradition, through an examination of the Anglo-American anti-monopoly tradition, as well as the ideas of Louis Brandeis and of the European Ordoliberals. And it shows these ideals at the height of their influence in the post-war era, a time of great prosperity and increasing equality. Finally, this book includes a programme for fighting the curse of bigness in our time, based on the premise that the democracies of the world need to provide better answers to their populations or face their own extinction.

1

WHERE OUR
PATH HAS LED

Once upon a time, the major industrialized nations
might have been thought to have learned their lesson.
After suffering communist and fascist revolutions, a
great depression and two catastrophic world wars, most
of the industrialized world changed its approach to the
economy and its role in a democracy.

Three extreme alternatives were rejected, at least
in their fullest forms: laissez-faire's rule by the
wealthy, communism's dictatorship of the proletariat
and fascism's state-directed capitalism. Instead, the
democratic nations of the world embarked on the
re-democratization of economic policy and the politics
of wealth redistribution. That path yielded decades of
economic growth that built strong middle classes who
enjoyed important freedoms and a previously unknown

level of prosperity, reducing what had become a massive gap between rich and poor.

To be sure, different parts of the world achieved widespread prosperity and freedom on different schedules. Large parts of the world – the 'Global South' – never made the gains hoped for. But the economic achievements of Western and Eastern democracies stole the thunder of both communism and fascism, whose calls for revolution were always driven by the unfairness and cruelty of unfettered capitalism.

No one economic policy overcame the inequalities produced by the Industrial Revolution and the consolidations of the early twentieth century. But anti-monopoly laws formed part of the story, by breaking the economic and political power of self-enriching trusts, and resisting the accumulation of wealth in monopoly and concentrated cartels. That was a mission reinforced by the horrible lessons of fascist Germany and Japan, and their close partnerships between government and private monopoly.

One way or another, concentration and inequality had its effects. In Great Britain, the country for which we have the most data, the share of income going to the top 5 per cent of wage earners had plunged to less than 20 per cent by the late 1970s.[1] In the United States, by the late 1960s, the share of national income going to the top 1 per cent of earners had fallen to 8 per cent.[2] France, Denmark, Japan and the Netherlands follow roughly similar trends.[3] Seemingly, the capitalist nations had found a way to square the circle, and by promising prosperity to the middle classes, presented an alluring alternative to the self-enriching dictatorships in other parts of the world.

That was then, and yet here we are again, as if trapped in a bad movie sequel. Laissez-faire economics, renamed neoliberalism, is the dominant economic ideology. And today, as in the 1910s, two essential economic facts characterize the industrialized world. The first is the re-emergence of an outrageous divide between the rich and the poor. The world's richest 1 per cent currently own 45 per cent of the world's wealth.[4] The world's ten richest billionaires own some $745 billion in combined wealth, a sum greater than the output of many nations.[5]

This trend is particularly stark in the United States and the United Kingdom, where the gains made in equality achieved by the 1970s have been lost. In the US, the top 1 per cent today earn 23.8 per cent of the national income and control an astonishing 38.6 per cent of national wealth. The top 0.1 per cent alone earn 12 per cent of the nation's income.[6]

The second feature is a return to concentrated economies – that is, industries that are dominated by fewer and larger companies, especially in the developed world. In 2015, the average market capitalization of the top hundred firms was a staggering seven thousand times that of the average for the bottom two thousand firms, whereas in 1995 it was just thirty-one times higher.[7] Similarly, since the year 2000, across US industries the measures of market concentration have increased in over 75 per cent of industries.[8]

The most visible manifestations of the consolidation trend sit right in front of our faces: the centralization of the once open and competitive tech industries into just a handful of giants, Facebook, Google, Apple and others, many of which have achieved monopolies not just in their home countries, but around the world, creating a rather extreme version of global economic monopoly.

The power that these companies wield underscores our sense of concern that the problems we face transcend the narrowly economic. Big tech is ubiquitous, knows too much about us, and seems to have too much power over what we see, hear, do, and even feel. It has reignited debates over who really rules, when the decisions of just a few people have such great influence over everyone.

Given a global economy that looks like that of the early twentieth century, is it any surprise that world politics has come to match it? The early twentieth century was marked by persistent economic distress, the brutal treatment of workers, the destruction of small- and medium-sized businesses, and broad economic suffering. That led to widespread popular anger and demands for something new, different and fairer. The economic distress experienced by broad swathes of the population subsequently led to communist revolutions in Russia and China, and to fascist or ultra-nationalist takeovers in Italy, Spain, Germany and Japan.

Today, economic grievances are again giving way to angry, populist and nationalist answers around the world. People are blaming their economic woes on immigrants, Jews, Muslims, Christians, the Chinese, or whomever, giving rise to a new generation of xenophobic, nationalist and racist politics. We have witnessed a return to the politics of outrage and violence, stoked by the humiliation of being poorer than one's own parents, and by the real prospect of falling through the cracks. We may be just one hard economic crash away from the end of democracy as we've known it.

The forgotten lesson from the twentieth century is that more measured, less angry alternatives work: programmes to aid the unemployed and the aged, to protect workers and labour movements, and to blunt the harshness and disparity inherent in unrestrained capitalism.

But that seems more obvious and better known. The missing piece of the puzzle is the importance of controlling economic structure, using laws designed to prevent or undo the consolidation of excessive private power. It would be an exaggeration to suggest that an anti-monopoly programme provides a full answer to inequality or other economic woes. But it does strike at the root cause of private political power – the economic concentration that facilitates political agency.

Advocating a revival of anti-monopoly laws is not meant to compete with other economic proposals aiming to address inequality. But laws that would redistribute wealth are often themselves blocked by the enhanced political power of concentrated industries, when they are able to exercise that power over democracy. In this way, the structure of the economy has an underlying influence on everything in the realm of economic policy.

All this is easier said than done. The world's largest and most powerful firms enjoy the kind of political influence that tends to dampen criticism. Many, moreover, are regarded as 'national champions' in their countries or regions of origin. And many countries encourage their champion to attempt the conquest of the rest of the world. It is very hard for any country to want to challenge the firms that it sees as its own champions, or of which an entire region is proud. Nor does any country or region want to feel it is unilaterally disarming. This is what makes the dilemma particularly difficult: we fear other giants, but often love our own.

The potential dangers of economic concentration and international consolidation can sometimes feel abstract and removed. We might gain a more concrete sense of the stakes by turning to the nation of Brazil, and the twenty-first-century story of the family slaughterhouse that grew into a global monopoly.

The Rise of a Global Meat Trust

In 1953, a Brazilian rancher named José Batista Sobrinho began his slaughterhouse operation in a straightforward fashion: by killing and butchering the cattle himself. He expanded into a modest, four-cow-a-day operation and found it to be a good business, and slowly but progressively expanded his holdings. By the year 2000, his firm, now known by his initials, JBS, was among the country's largest beef slaughterhouses, but it remained a private, family-owned operation. The founding family liked to emphasize their country roots and their traditional methods of management. As Wesley Batista, one of the founder's sons, put it in 2011, the firm was run in a 'a simple way', without 'a lot of layers, not a lot of fancy things, not a lot of time spent on PowerPoint presentations'.[9]

In the early twenty-first century, effective control of JBS passed from the father, José, to two of his sons, Wesley and Joesley, then ambitious young men in their thirties. The younger generation of Batista brothers had different and far grander visions than their father did. Coming of age amidst the exciting prospects of globalization and Brazil's emergence as South America's most promising economy, they began to see a way they might refashion their family business into something much larger, a global empire of meat.

It wasn't just that. The Batistas also sensed a golden opportunity to propel their family, already very rich in Brazilian terms, into the ranks of the ultra-wealthy, the ludicrously rich, and to become the Brazilian equivalent of the Trumps, Boehringers or Kwoks, the billionaire families emerging in the United States, Europe and Asia. The story of how they did so, and what happened, is the economic story of our times.

* * *

In 2005, soon after taking control of the family company, the young Batista brothers first met with a man named Guido Mantega, then president of the Brazilian Development Bank. The Development Bank is a branch of the Brazilian government with the power to lend out money at subsidized rates. It had been designed to help small and medium-sized businesses catch up with the big guys, by providing credit to invest in domestic projects. But Mantega, an economist, politician and apostle of globalization, saw that as old-fashioned.

Mantega discussed with the brothers a different plan to refashion the family business. Instead of building up the business the old way, they agreed on a much faster alternative: acquiring other firms – buying out as many as possible of the world's other major meat processors.

Buying companies is expensive: where would the money come from? That's where Mantega and his Development Bank came in. In the early 2000s, the Brazilian government, infatuated with globalism and global markets, was eager to create a new generation of so-called global players. President Luiz Inácio Lula da Silva and his Workers' Party, under the banner of globalization, would use Brazilian money to build companies that invested outside of Brazil. What that meant, in practice, was cheap money from Mantega's Development Bank to buy rival companies in other countries.

Mantega and the Batista brothers conducted a trial run of the new strategy in neighbouring Argentina. That nation's leading slaughterhouse, Swift Armour SA, had been weakened by Argentina's seemingly never-ending financial crisis and was vulnerable to a buyout at a cheap price. Mantega was enthusiastic and approved the financing of a $200 million purchase at discount interest rates. The brothers were also asked to wire $3.2 million in US dollars to an overseas account. It was what one might call a personal expression of gratitude. 'That's what it took for us to get the deal done,' said the elder Batista later.[10]

And so the trial run was a happy one for everyone. Over the next decade, the Batista brothers would return over and over again to the Brazilian Development Bank, embarking on what amounted to a state-backed global spending spree, lubricated by large cash bribes. Armed with billions in public, risk-free loans, and later shareholder money, the Batista brothers set their eyes on other targets. In the late 2000s, they bought, in quick succession, three American firms weakened by the Great Recession: Swift, the beef division of Smithfield Foods and Pilgrim's.

After buying its main domestic rival and some of Australia's slaughterhouses, JBS had managed to make itself into the largest beef processor in the world. It was by then slaughtering some ninety thousand cattle a day and exporting beef to over 150 countries.[11] Using the miracles of cheap credit and consolidation, the sons had achieved more apparent growth in six years than their father had in fifty years of hard work.

When the time came, the Batistas did not neglect themselves or their immediate family. In 2009, they conducted an initial public offering of shares in the family firm, while holding on to a controlling share. The stock sale was a success, propelling the Batistas into the growing new cadre of twenty-first-century billionaires. By 2014, the family had a combined net worth of $4.3 billion, joining the ranks of other Brazilian billionaire clans that then included the Marinho family ($28.9 billion) and the Safras ($20 billion), among others. Ironically, the build-up of wealth by these families occurred during a time when many thought Brazil was teaching the world a lesson on how to combat inequality.

If they had been satisfied to be merely the world's largest beef processor, or merely wealthy, the Batistas might have avoided some of what was soon to befall them. But growth is addictive, and only a few executives really understand the dangers of bigness, or know when to stop, until it is too late for everyone. To be fair to the Batistas, it must have been hard to stop when both the Brazilian government and private sources of capital welcomed and applauded JBS's plans to go further. Through the 2010s, JBS began buying chicken and pork processors around the world, in Mexico, Australia and other countries. They made a total of more than forty further acquisitions, which would make JBS not just the world's largest meat processor, but the second-largest food company in the world (after Nestlé).[12]

At this stage JBS's buying spree began to cause a chain reaction around the globe, as it triggered similar consolidation campaigns by other meat processors, eager to divide up what were now being called the 'protein markets'. JBS's rivals now included China's WH Group, which relied on Chinese state subsidies to buy American pork producer Smithfield Foods for $4.7 billion. Not to be left out, American giant Tyson Foods, the inventor of the vertically integrated 'factory-farm' model of chicken production, went on its own buying spree.

In the anti-monopoly tradition, government is supposed to block mergers that lead to monopoly or reduce competition significantly. Yet somehow the consolidation of the world's meat processing industry slid under the radar. With one exception, in the United States, the world's governments, over twenty years, did almost nothing to slow down or prevent the acquisitions of JBS or the other global consolidators. To the contrary, government was, instead, encouraging concentration and consolidation, at least by their favoured champions. And among them, the Brazilian government was the most generous of all. When it was all said and done,

Brazilian taxpayers had ultimately backed a $20 billion global spending spree.

In consequence, by the mid-2010s, the global markets for beef, chicken and pork had been transformed. Meat processing, once a largely regional business, was now dominated by a small number of firms. The effect was to change how the spoils were divided, or if you prefer, the carcass butchered. In the new order, a small, consolidated group of middlemen – the meat processors – were in a position to squeeze suppliers and retailers to enhance their profits. The losers were small and medium-sized ranchers, smaller retailers, workers and, of course, the animals.

It may be no surprise to learn that industry concentration has led to wage stagnation and a widespread squeezing of ranchers and farmers around the world. Even as demand for meat goes up, the actual producers, and the people who raise the animals, have seen their share of profits diminish. JBS was not particularly concerned with such matters. In fact, a 2017 investigation found that JBS bought from suppliers in Brazil whose work practices included work hours of up to twenty hours a day, and the use of rotten meat to feed employees.[13]

As for the animals, consolidation brought the spread of 'factory' techniques, first developed to maximize chicken yield, to the raising of cattle and pigs, a trend sometimes referred to as the 'chickenification' of cattle and pork. Compared with earlier times, all of the animals now live in smaller spaces, in much larger production facilities. They are treated with more drugs, and their lives are shorter, thanks to the use of growth hormones that ensure a more rapid attainment of the ideal weight for slaughtering. All of this does reduce the cost of creating a gram of protein, but it is the animals who pay the price.

But if bigness has been bad for the little guys, workers and animals, aren't consumers at least better off? Unfortunately, even this did not go as expected. Industry rationalization did result in a decrease in prices for protein over the 1990s and early 2000s. But since then, prices have stabilized, and as consolidation has increased, even begun increasing for pork and beef. Increasing demand is part of the picture but another, obvious reason is bargaining power. With just three or four dominant meat processors in each country, it is easy to set higher prices. In fact, together they can decide how animals will be raised, what they will pay for cattle, and at what price they will sell meat to retailers.

The story of the industry's economics is important, but not the full story. For the effects of excessive bigness are rarely limited to economic redistribution, but have a nasty tendency to spill over into politics, particularly, into the corruption of government and the creation of political backlash. And unfortunately for Brazil, its reckless globalization campaign would soon shake the nation to its foundations.

In 2016, the Brazilian federal police force conducted a raid of JBS's offices.[14] The raids confirmed what was long suspected: that JBS and other firms had been routinely paying off health inspectors to avoid complying with Brazil's food safety laws and inflate their margins. The firms, the police alleged, had used bribes to hide the alteration of spoilage dates and to facilitate the export of potentially rotten or disease-ridden meat, treated with chemical additives to disguise odours and appearance. At a widely reported press conference, an investigator even accused the meat processing industry of selling rotten meat, disguised with a carcinogenic acid treatment, to Brazilian schoolchildren.

Soon after the tainted beef scandal, the Batista brothers were arrested by a different prosecutor after accidentally sending prosecutors a tape of a conversation discussing bribes with Brazilian president Michel Temer. Over the course of that prosecution the brothers would admit to having bribed over 1,800 politicians and officials. The investigations revealed, among other things, that JBS had, for years, knowingly violated rainforest protection laws. Overall, the brothers would eventually admit to paying $150 million in bribes and 'contributions'.[15] Guido Mantega, the man who originally financed JBS's buying spree, was also arrested on an allegation of taking bribes during this period, but was never charged.

These tainted meat and corruption scandals were not good for JBS or for the nation of Brazil. In 2017, countries around the world announced bans on the import of Brazilian meat, creating a near collapse of the sector. That collapse dovetailed with severe problems and scandals being faced by other Brazilian 'national champions' in the 2010s, including the petroleum firm Petrobras, the mining firm Vale and the aircraft manufacturer Embraer, among others. These were the heavily subsidized global champions that were supposed to be transforming Brazil in the global economy of the future, yet each of them faced both corruption scandals and severe business problems based on a pattern of over-expansion and dubious investments.

It turned out, in retrospect, that the Brazilian government had bet heavily on a small number of giant firms, so long as those firms were willing to wire cash to overseas accounts or contribute to political campaigns in a generous fashion. One study revealed that a majority of the Brazilian Development Bank's loans went not to small and medium business, as intended, but instead to the richest and largest firms.[16]

When those firms began to weaken, and in some cases collapse, they took the economy with them.

By 2014, Brazil had entered its worst recession in decades. The economy contracted by almost 10 per cent, and unemployment rose by 76 per cent, producing twelve million newly unemployed, angry workers, and an alarming rise in crime rates.[17] The bet on globalization and consolidation had seemed like a good idea in the 2000s, and in more moderate forms might have succeeded. But a company like JBS was really doing little else than spending the Brazilian public's money to destroy competition, both at home and overseas, so as to squeeze the profits of ranchers in the United States, Australia and other countries. That strategy produced growth for a while, but ultimately resulted in a stunning and destructive collapse.

Among other achievements, Brazil's progress in combatting inequality turned out to be far less impressive than advertised. In retrospect, during the booming 2000s, the poorest labourers did improve their lot, and reforms like higher minimum wage had their impact. But the wealthiest, like the Batistas, got even wealthier, making inequality worse. And when the crash did come it hit the poorest hardest of all, undoing much of the progress of the previous decade and adding 6.3 million to the ranks of the impoverished, who grew to total 11 per cent of the population. Unemployment was stuck at over 12 per cent, a number that refused to come back down. In this way Brazil became this era's defining example of what the Curse of Bigness looks like, especially considering what happened next.

For Brazil's economic misery would soon transform its politics. Two decades of wealth consolidation in the nation's elite and wealthy created a nationalist backlash of ferocious power, a danger for any democracy. Brazil had been an authoritarian dictatorship from 1964 through 1984. In 2018, with the economy still suffering, a former military officer, following the old script, ran for president as a national saviour who would restore Brazilian greatness. Jair Bolsonaro adopted as his slogan an unsubtle echo of German's old 'über alles' anthem: 'Brazil above everything, God above everyone'.[18] He promised to re-establish Brazil's military power, create economic stability and wage war on the various villains: the 'reds', gays and other scapegoats. Bolsonaro promised to 'break the system'. And, of course, he won election easily.

The story of JBS and Brazil shows that we have not absorbed the important lessons of twentieth-century history. For Brazil's progress, through economic consolidation, to stark inequality, to economic collapse and extremist government, is hardly unprecedented. It shows that what we need, most of all, is to relearn the hard-won lessons of the 1930s, the rise of fascism and the Second World War.

2

THE LOST LESSONS
OF THE SECOND
WORLD WAR

In the years after the Second World War, with millions dead and major cities in ruins, the major nations of the world began to ask a pressing question. Just how might they prevent the rise of fascism again? What could stop just a few factions in a few nations from pitching the entire world into a devastating world war?

There were several answers to that question. The United Nations was founded in 1945, with a Charter banning international aggression, its self-described mandate to 'save succeeding generations from the scourge of war, which twice in our lifetime has brought untold sorrow to mankind'. Special limits were imposed on Germany and Japan to prevent their redevelopment of military power. The Bretton Woods institutions – the IMF, the World Bank and the WTO – were founded to prevent international economic instability and the kinds of trade wars that had preceded the military wars.

But we have forgotten a critical piece of this puzzle: the targeting of the economic origins of fascism. Few now remember the efforts to break the economic structures of Germany and Japan, based on concerns that they were the catalysts for dictatorship. But as Walter Bennett of the American Justice Department argued at the time, 'Nothing provides a finer weapon for the budding dictator than a concentration of economic power which he can take over at the top.'[19]

In fact, in the immediate aftermath of World War II, the breaking of German and Japanese industrial monopoly was seen as essential. In the words of a US Senate report, 'the structure and control of German industry must be so altered. . . to crush German imperialism permanently and thus permit a peaceful and democratic Germany to arise.'[20] Accordingly, after the fall of the Third Reich, the Allies did not just disband the Nazi government and army, but also broke up the major German monopoly corporations. They did so specifically so that they could not be 'used by Germany as instruments of political or economic aggression', in the words of the law.[21] Similarly, in Japan, the American occupation broke down power of the *zaibatsu* – the major conglomerates that dominated the Japanese economy.

To be fair, it was not just Japan and Germany that had, in the interwar years, come to tolerate extensive monopolization of their economies. The period of the late 1920s through to the 1930s was perhaps unmatched in its breathless worship of corporate size and power, with Mussolini and Stalin serving as important apostles of centralized planning. During this time, not just Germany, but nations like Britain, France and Canada had begun to tolerate the existence of monopolies and cartels. In Britain, the historic home of anti-monopoly principle, the 1919 Report on Trusts announced that ninety-three 'quasi-monopoly' associations were extant.[22] Even the United States, home to the world's most aggressive anti-monopoly laws, would give up on enforcement over the 1920s, and, in the early 1930s, in a failed attempt to recover from the Depression, it would embrace central planning and the wholesale suspension of its laws.

The truth is that by the early 1930s the entire world suffered from the Curse of Bigness. The major nations had nurtured and chosen their own monopolists and national champions, a path that would lead to economic collapse and world war. At the same time, the world tolerated extraordinary international cartelization – that is, webs of international agreements that were most often agreements not to invade the territory of national monopolists. We see echoes of this in the design of some of today's multinationals, which preserve the sense of international competition while destroying much of the benefit intended to be passed on to consumers or workers.

We can focus our efforts by taking a closer look at the most extreme examples: those of Germany and Japan, as they transformed into expansionist authoritarian powers.

Pre-war German Cartels and the Nazi Economy

Here is how Senator Harley Kilgore summarized matters in 1944: Germany 'built up a great series of industrial monopolies in steel, rubber, coal and other materials. The monopolies soon got control of Germany, brought Hitler to power and forced virtually the whole world into war.'[23]

That statement is unquestionably an exaggeration. But looking back, it is hard to deny that the economic ideology and structure of Weimar and then Nazi Germany played a role both in Hitler's ability to consolidate power, and to transform the German state into a command economy designed for warfare. This is a story that we must understand to see the risks we are taking today.

The story starts in the nineteenth century, when, as in other parts of the industrialized world, German firms began growing in size and scope, and began to form cartels. What were these cartels? They were industry-wide organizations – like the steel cartel, the Stahlwerksverband – that acted to coordinate industry pricing, product quality and other relevant matters. The more advanced cartels were more like umbrella companies that closely monitored the industry and policed any violations of its rules. Depending on the degree of coordination, a German cartel therefore tended to fuse the industry into something that was technically short of a monopoly but replicated many of its features.

In contrast to Britain and the United States, German intellectuals and the German state were nearly unanimous in their acceptance and even celebration of the cartels. Gustav Schmoller, an economic historian of immense influence in the early twentieth century, championed the *kartellen* as 'a new order of public life'. The cartels were a brilliant German invention, an improvement on the nastiness of British industrialization. To their supporters, they 'represented a progressive stage in the order of national economy, progress which would inevitably lead to a more highly organized form of the national economy'.[24]

Part of the German intellectual embrace of the cartel reflected a broader tendency in German thought that accepted the exertion of power and the triumph of the strong over the weak as inevitable and indeed ultimately beneficent. But if 'übermensch' was a German coinage, it echoed the broader tenets of Social Darwinism, which, at the time, enjoyed great currency among the global capitalist class as a political philosophy, and for some, something of a religion.

Circa 1900, the faith was this: humanity was in the midst of an evolutionary transformation whose goal was nothing less than the forging of a new man. To make way, it was necessary to displace the weak, the small and the old-fashioned, so as to make room for the new, the scientific and, above all, the great and strong. In business this meant a pure laissez-faire capitalism that cheered on the displacement of small or traditional business with mighty monopoly corporations or cartels, thought to be miracles of modern science. In politics, it meant opposition to any interventions that might be thought to stop the strong from displacing the weak. Hence opposition to 'poor laws' in Britain, on the premise that the impoverished should be left to live or die on their own, so as 'to clear the world of them, and make room for better'.[25] In matters of social planning, the Social Darwinists supported eugenics campaigns meant to cull the physically and mentally disabled, and thereby help speed up the coming of the new age. John D. Rockefeller Jr. would personally fund an initiative to sterilize some fifteen million Americans. As Herbert Spencer put it, 'The forces which are working out the great scheme of perfect happiness. . . exterminate such sections of mankind as stand in their way, with the same sternness that they exterminate beasts of prey and herds of useless ruminants.'[26]

As this suggests, all the industrialized nations had their own monopoly movements, and all of them faced industrial transformation. But here we must dwell on a major difference between the German and American story.

To people alive today, the United States seems the epitome of unrestrained capitalism. But things were not this way in the nineteenth century, when it remained primarily agricultural, and big business was relatively new and distrusted by the public. In early-twentieth-century America, the wealthy 'robber barons' (as they were labelled) ran into intellectual, popular and legal resistance from a progressive movement spurred on by journalists (the 'muck rakers') and anchored by figures like Theodore Roosevelt and Louis Brandeis (to whom we turn later in this book).

In the progressive backlash against the monopolies (known as the antitrust movement), the original and most powerful trust corporations, like Standard Oil, were broken up. Other major monopolizers, like the famous banker J. P. Morgan, died in a state of public disgrace. This is not to say that the forces of opposition in the United States won every battle. But the ideological and political resistance had a major impact.

Turn of the century Germany was a very different story, for there was little political or popular resistance to the de facto monopolization of the German economy. Instead, German intellectuals tended to bask in the superiority of German industry, while emphasizing its more civilized aspects, and this blindness to the risks is what made it so dangerous. The great intellectual Gustav Schmoller proclaimed the superiority of the German way: the American monopolies were 'a system of robbery and fraud', while the German cartels promoted 'a system of justice and equity'.[27] Writing in 1934, historian Hermann Levy would note that 'the word "monopoly" has never acquired any popular meaning in German economic terminology', and that 'no "anti-monopolistic" spirit or reasoning can be found among the German masses.'[28]

As this may suggest, patriotism and nationalism contributed to the German support for its cartels. Many Germans saw their industrial leaders as engaged in a great struggle with British, French and American companies for a fair share of the spoils of empire. As Knut Wolfgang Nörr wrote, 'the cartels acted as industrial fighting organizations against foreign competitors.'[29]

Where the intellectuals and public went, so did the state. In 1923, the Weimar Republic passed a law explicitly legalizing and regulating cartels, accepting, with a few exceptions, mergers designed to produce industry-wide monopolies (known in Germany as 'rationalizations'). By the mid-1920s, the German economy, especially heavy industry, was organized and concentrated in a relatively small number of monopolies and tight cartels. Among those that would prove important in the Nazi economy were the Krupp armament company; the Siemens conglomerate; Vereinigte Stahlwerke A.G., the monopolist controlling mining, iron and steel; and the infamous IG Farben chemical company, manufacturer of the poison gas used in the Holocaust, which merged to monopoly in 1925.

The price of German acceptance and glorification of its monopolized and cartelized economy became clearer in the 1930s. To be sure, historians have long debated the degree and extent to which the major German cartels and monopoly firms were accomplices or victims in the process of Nazification. But what seems far more obvious is that Germany's economic structure contributed to and created some of the conditions for a transition into dictatorship. We can consider four ways: by contributing to the severity of the German depression; through heavy industry's role as an aid to Hitler's consolidation of power in the early

1930s; in the transformation of the German economy into a command economy; and finally in the specific role played by German monopolists in the war effort.

Adolf Hitler first gained measurable electoral power in the 1930 elections, when, in the midst of a brutal depression, he rode a wave of widespread economic and social anger. He was not the first to do so and would not be the last. But Hitler's evil brilliance lay in his ability to both ride the popular anger created by corporate misfeasance, while simultaneously, if more quietly, promising industrial leaders that which they wanted most.

The German depression of the early 1930s was made worse by the rigid structure of the German economy, and it 'caused the ruined masses of the German middle class to follow a leader who knew how to fight his social decline by donning a field-grey uniform. . .' The German depression, in other words, created a 'fertile ground on which mass fascism grew'. But if German heavy industry did not intend the depression, it would eventually come to a far more direct contribution to the Nazi Party's consolidation of power, by throwing its support behind Hitler's party when its hold on power was most tenuous.

The courtship between the Nazi Party and German heavy industry was neither rapid nor uncomplicated.

Through the 1920s, and even into the early 1930s, industry remained unsympathetic, indeed resistant, to the Nazi pitch. The party was comprised of some fairly wild fringe figures, like Hitler himself, that tended to alienate business elites. But as the 1930s went on, Hermann Göring, the chief recruiter of the 'circle of friends' for the Nazi cause, would find a growing number of business leaders willing to agree that democracy had failed. They were open to the idea that what the German economy really needed, as Göring proposed, was a strong hand on the levers of power.

Here's how one of the organizers of the secret meetings with the Nazis in the early 1930s put it: 'The general aim of the industrialists at that time, was to see a strong leader come to power in Germany who could form a government which would long remain in power.' More than anything, industry feared continued instability, labour unrest, and most of all, the possibility of a communist revolution. In the words of George Hallgarten, industry decided it was best to support 'Hitler as the lesser of two evils' and was 'eager to make the best of his coming to power, both politically and economically'.

The key period was late 1932, when the Nazi Party, having gained a measure of power, began to face serious setbacks. As the economy began to recover, the Nazis lost supporters, began losing seats, and also faced their own bankruptcy. In another version of history, the Nazi movement might have just been one of those short-lived aberrations that all democracies occasionally suffer through. But it was in that year that heavy industry decisively turned its back on democracy. Key leaders effectively accepted the Nazi Party's promise to save Germany from socialism and the unions, abandoning more moderate conservatives who still believed in democracy and the Weimar Republic. One is struck by how the decisions of just a few men could transform Germany and throw the entire world into war.

And so, as the Nazi Party tottered in 1932, the industrialists, previously divided and moderate, offered major financial support to the Nazis in their hour of greatest need. This was manifested by the 'circle of friends' becoming the main financial backers of the Nazi Party. In November 1932, they distributed millions of marks to Hitler and his SS units while also assuming the debts of the party. By the end of 1933, one firm, IG Farben, the chemical monopolist, would give the Nazis 4.5 million Reichsmarks. The Nazi Party used the money to fund the disruption of ongoing elections with its paramilitary forces and massive propaganda campaigns, in a successful effort to cripple the democratic process.

There was more to Hitler's rise than financial backing and co-opting of any industry resistance.

The conservative leaders of the time cannot be spared blame: their underestimation of Nazi ruthlessness and foolish hopes of co-opting Hitler by giving him power were mistakes whose notoriety is well deserved. But what cannot be denied is that the concentration of the German economy into so few controllers of industry also made it much easier for Hitler to gain support, and once support came, for it to make a big difference.

The concentrated structure of the German economy also made it easier for Hitler to transform Germany into a command economy, a war machine. After gaining total power in 1933, Hitler himself drafted a proposal for a four-year economic plan which emphasized industrialization for military purposes. He wrote: 'The extent of the military development of our resources cannot be too large, nor its pace too swift,'[30] and also stated that the purpose of the economy was 'Germany's self-assertion and the extension of her Lebensraum'.[31]

Key to executing this plan was *Lenkungslehre*, the doctrine of economic control which relied on the cartels and monopolies. The Nazi Party called its invention a new form of economic government, the 'capitalist planned economy', which preserved private property rights but gave the state the right to intervene whenever it saw fit: directing the steel industry to build plating suitable for panzer tanks, the chemical monopolist to develop synthetic rubber for war uses, and so on. Hence the observation that Germany's cartels and monopolies proved 'agile and dangerous pacemakers for the transformation of a free market into an authoritarian market'.[32]

Finally, we come to the role of German industry in the war itself. This was a subject of intensive study by the Allies after the conflict. Suffice to say that United Steel, Krupp, Siemens, IG Farben and other major German companies became virtual arms of the German state, and also beneficiaries of both the military build-up and of war. As a US Army official asserted of Farben, for example, it 'serve[d] the German state as one of the principal industrial cores around which successive German drives for world conquest were organized'.[33] The Krupp armament company, run by Alfried Krupp von Bohlen und Halbach, was another major beneficiary of the German rearmament and the subsequent war. It was the biggest manufacturer of large-calibre artillery, armour plate, large field artillery, and also, the largest private builder of U-boats and warships.

As the Nuremberg trials would later establish, executives at Krupp and other firms did profit from the use of slave labour, both concentration camp labour and tens of thousands of French prisoners of war. IG Farben, for its part, actually operated a rubber plant in the Auschwitz complex, as well as operating its own concentration camp (for reasons of efficiency), while supplying the Zyklon B gas used to kill over a million captives.

Nonetheless, as the German corporations were clearly the subject of orders from the Nazi state, it has often been argued that it is wrong to blame the state monopolies for what happened. In the end, whether the great German corporations were willing accomplices or victims of Hitler's rule does not really matter. What we want to know is something different: whether the structure of the German economy was dangerously facilitative of the establishment and conduct of the Nazi state. The historical record gives strong reason to suggest that the extreme concentration of German industry before the war was an aid to Hitler's rise to power and facilitated Germany's effort to take over the world. That is the lesson that cannot be ignored in our times.

Japan and the *Zaibatsu*

The industrial history of Japan over the early twentieth century was distinct. As in Germany, there was no effort to control the rise of concentrated business; indeed, quite the opposite. With the exception of the communist states, the entwining of Japanese industry and the state was arguably more extensive than in any other industrialized nation. The lines that might usually be thought to separate government and the private sector were crossed in Japan in a manner that makes the head spin.

Both Imperial Japan and the Third Reich allowed a concentration and consolidation of their economies. But Japan provides a lesson in what can happen in a nation bereft of real avenues of popular resistance, and of the intense entwining of public and private functions. If there is one present-day country that pre-war Japan may give insight into, it is China, with a similar lack of checks on power and a blurred line between public and private.

The pre-war Japanese economic order was centred on the *zaibatsu* – a series of industrial combinations run by powerful family dynasties. The *zaibatsu* bore some similarities to American and European syndicates, trusts and cartels, but were different in other ways. Two stand out. Unlike the American trusts, the Japanese *zaibatsu* did not tend to each monopolize a single industry (on the model of America's Standard Oil, or Germany's IG Farben etc.), but instead covered enormous numbers of industries in a conglomerate fashion. Hence, for a given industry (say, tractors), there remained competition – sometimes fierce – among the *zaibatsu* at least. This crossed over into the political system, where different *zaibatsu* were allied with different political parties, and also separately with the army and navy. That said, the *zaibatsu* nonetheless concentrated economic power in a manner that exceeded the American and European examples in several ways.

By the mid-twentieth century, a big four of Sumitomo, Mitsui, Mitsubishi and Yasuda dominated the Japanese economy, and collectively, the ten largest *zaibatsu* accounted for most of the economy. Unlike in Europe and America, the *zaibatsu* also ran the Japanese banking and finance system. Their joint control over credit could be wielded to create almost unsurmountable barriers to entry for would-be challengers. Finally, while some public shares were issued to raise money, majority ownership of the pre-war *zaibatsu* remained firmly in the hands of the family dynasty, in an extraordinary concentration of decision-making power. As Professor Young Namkoong writes, 'The technology and the form of business used by the *zaibatsu* were modern but the substance of the interpersonal and interfirm relations was essentially that of the hierarchical familism of traditional Japan.'[34]

The most important lesson for our time, however, comes from the degree to which the power of the Japanese firms went beyond mere economic matters and freely extended to politics and civilian government.

To give some measure of their influence, the Mitsui and Mitsubishi *zaibatsu* each sponsored its own political party. The two parties, Rikken Seiyūkai and Rikken Minseitō, generally took turns forming the government with their own prime ministers. This is not necessarily to suggest that the *zaibatsu* ruled pre-war Japan, but rather that the relationship between the great conglomerates and the civilian government was extremely intimate. As Professor Namkoong writes, 'The relationship between government and business in pre-war Japan cannot be understood within the framework of the modern Western distinction between public and private sectors. To pre-war Japanese political and business leaders, the line of demarcation did not exist in any philosophical or ideological sense.'[35]

None of this is, however, to suggest that the *zaibatsu* were all-powerful. To comprehend the balance of power in pre-war Japan is to understand the independence and power of other branches of government, including the Imperial Army and Imperial Navy, and the Emperor and his bureaucratic staff. The bottom line is that the *zaibatsu* were a key part of government earlier on, and their interests and appetite for monopoly profits were among the great drivers of Japan's interests.

Japan, unlike Germany, did not explicitly adopt a particularized ideology of progress that favoured monopolization or cartelization. It might be more accurate to say that the powerful, indeed dominant ideology of pre-war Japan would make it the duty of the *zaibatsu* – and of everyone – to maximize the power and greatness of the Japanese Empire.

Here's how the president of the great Mitsubishi conglomerate, among the most powerful, put things in 1920: 'We must never lose sight of the fact that while we pursue material objectives in our enterprises we also strive for spiritual goals. . . [T]he growth or decline of production is intimately related to the prosperity or decline of the nation and to the cultural progress of society.' Hence, 'it must remain the supreme goal of management of our enterprises that they serve the country first, it is our ideal to exert all our energies in the pursuit of this ultimate goal.'[36]

Viewed in retrospect, another striking fact about pre-war Japan was the near-total absence of strong public counterweights to the private–public union of power – resistance as might be provided by an anti-monopoly movement, strong labour unions, a strong middle class, or by small and medium-sized businesses. According to Corwin Edwards, the *zaibatsu*-run economy produced conditions ripe for Japan's aggression as it created 'semi-feudal relations between employer and employee, held down wages, and blocked the development of labor unions'. For decades, the conglomerates 'retarded the rise of a

Japanese middle class', which he believed was essential to 'humanitarian sentiments' and a 'counterweight to military design'.[37]

That the separation of powers, such as it was, came from the independence of the army and navy says something.

Despite Japan's distinct system, its descent into extremist nationalism followed a familiar script. In the early 1930s, in the midst of economic hardship, Japan's most radical and dangerous military leaders purported to turn on the *zaibatsu*, blaming them for the nation's problems, and insisting that they further pledge their allegiance to the military state and obey its orders. But at the same time, the military was also opening new markets for conquest. In time, the *zaibatsu* would become essential allies of the imperial state. As in Germany, the *zaibatsu* would later claim that they were victims of forces beyond their control – yet at the same time, their very structure was essential to Japan's war effort.

It is true that some of the *zaibatsu* might have preferred a more peaceful conquest of foreign markets, and it is also true that it was the Imperial Army and Navy, as opposed to the civilian government, who spearheaded the most aggressive overseas expansion. But it is also hard to deny that the *zaibatsu* profited mightily from the occupation and colonization of much of East Asia. A study led by Corwin Edwards concluded that the *zaibatsu* were among the 'groups principally responsible for the war and. . . a principal factor in the Japanese war potential'.[38]

International Cartels

Japan and Germany offer stark lessons in the dangers of consolidation followed by economic depression. But there was more. Imagine if, in our times, Volkswagen, Fiat, General Motors, Ford, Toyota and other major car manufacturers were to agree to stay out of the others' countries. Hence, the United States would belong to GM and Ford; Italy to Fiat; Japan to Toyota and Honda; and so on.

There is no doubt that would be a rather different world than the one we live in, and as we shall see, it creates further dangers. But that was the state of affairs caused by international cartelization over the 1920s and 1930s, when a private economic order was created by a large web of international cartels, based on agreements between dominant firms or the cartels themselves, sometimes backed by policing organizations. We ought to watch closely to see if today's global multinationals are effectively replicating these very dangerous conditions.

As suggested above, the typical substance of an international cartel agreement was simply to stay away from the others' territory. More advanced cartels divided up world markets more completely, or dictated production or pricing levels, as enforced by some kind of international body. The most advanced became themselves true international monopolies, predecessors of the global monopolies of our times.

The international cartels themselves took several forms. They were sometimes 'cartels of cartels' – for example, an agreement between German and British trade associations, like the International Railmakers' Association (IRMA). Others were agreements between the monopolists or dominant firms of each of the major countries – an agreement among giants – as in the example of the international rayon (or artificial silk) industry. In resource industries, the international cartels were typically designed to make sure the price of some raw material, like tin, or oil, stayed at a certain level.

The most important effect of these cartels was to limit the impact on pricing or quality that might have been encouraged by competition from imports, as the car example shows. In some sense, while the protectionist trade policies of the early 1930s are often blamed for making the global depression worse, it must also be understood that international cartelization had the same effect; indeed, it operated not as a tariff, but actually a total barrier to trade.

After the war came to an end, the international cartels faced widespread blame, sometimes in very strong terms. A report issued by the American Senate in 1944 stated that 'the rapid growth of cartels during the late 1920's and early 1930's coincided with the onset of a world-wide depression [which] led to the adoption of Nazi totalitarianism.'[39] The *New Republic* decried a 'Corporate International', 'an octopus that crosses international boundaries and straddles the world'.[40] The theory was that Germany had used its influence over international cartels intentionally to weaken the ability of the Allies to build up their armies before the war.

It is sometimes said that trade ties help prevent war, by giving countries a sense of economic interdependence. Whether that is true or not, it is nonetheless important to examine if today's global monopolies, which control the major firms in each country, might create similar problems, trigger the anger of populist nationalistic movements, and once again threaten the security of the world.

Clearly the economic structure of the 1920s and 1930s contributed to the rise of dangerous governments around the world. But at the same time, the rise of private giants fostered an intellectual and popular reaction, both in the United States and Europe. This gave birth to an anti-monopoly tradition which would become quite powerful – and whose lessons we need to relearn today.

3

THE ANTI-MONOPOLY TRADITION

This book aims to restore the tradition that sought to break the excessive private power threatening democracy and individual liberty. But what is this tradition? And who were its proponents?

The history of twentieth-century thought, in matters of economics, is often depicted as a grand struggle between the new ideologies of communism (represented by Marx, Lenin and Mao) and fascism (Mussolini, Franco and Hitler), and the slightly older traditions of capitalist democracy.

But there's a different story over the same time period. It is one that can be called the battle over monopoly and central planning. It was waged between the forces that supported and embraced monopolization, and those who fought it, tried to break it, slow it, or in some way maintain some separation of powers in the economy. And when you see things this way, the history looks different. For it turns out that the communists, fascists and extreme capitalists all favoured the monopoly structure, and planning over competition. All of these forces believed in the triumph of the monopoly form and also that it was a natural triumph of the strong over the weak. It was capitalists like Rockefeller and J. P. Morgan who proclaimed competition outdated, and it was Vladimir Lenin whose central planning was an imitation of monopoly industry.

The resistance to these forces came from a different place, a tradition that had long resisted excessive size, while maintaining the link between individual freedom and control over private power. In this chapter, we examine a movement that sought a middle way between unfettered capitalism and complete socialism and attempted to preserve an economy that retained some democratic distribution of economic power.

It is a story that begins a long time ago, with the resistance to the economic tyranny of the Queen of England, or more precisely, her decision to give a monopoly on playing cards to her groom.

The British Common Law

Queen Elizabeth I, who ruled England from 1558 to 1603, is usually remembered for her personal eccentricities, and perhaps most of all for her long reign. But she was also a monopolizer extraordinaire, and in that way, the unintended inspiration for the anti-monopoly tradition.

Late in her reign, in the last years of the sixteenth century, the Queen began to indulge heavily in the use of a royal prerogative known as the Crown monopoly. Monopoly grants were originally used by the Crown to encourage invention and industry (like today's patents), but Elizabeth used them in a more arbitrary way, as a kind of royal favour meant to reward her friends and political patrons. Her monopolies would come to cover a broad scope of the English economy, including such fundamentals as the sale of salt. 'Elizabeth lavished them [monopolies], with a munificent hand . . .' wrote a nineteenth-century American jurist '[until] All trade and commerce, whether foreign or domestic, was appropriated by monopolists. Industry and the arts languished alike, under these unnatural restraints and fictitious embarrassments.'[41]

The Queen's monopoly grants were, understandably, resented by merchants and the public, who took their grievances to the common law courts. An important test case arose out of Elizabeth's 1598 grant of a monopoly over the import and sale of playing cards to her groom, a man named Edward Darcy. Thomas Allin, a member of a medieval guild, the Worshipful

Company of Haberdashers, decided to challenge the law by selling his own cards. That set up the famous *Case of Monopolies*, in which the leading English court of the day pronounced the Queen's monopoly 'utterly void' as 'against the common law'.[42] (To protect the Queen's honour, the court said she must have been deceived when she gave out the monopoly.) Facing insurrection, Elizabeth agreed to revoke some of the most restrictive monopolies.

However important the principle announced may have been, the ruling did not stop James I, Elizabeth's successor, from indulging in the monopoly habit. Parliament in 1624 enacted the English 'Statute of Monopolies', which banned monopoly in strong terms, declaring that 'all monopolies. . . are altogether contrary to the Laws of this Realm, and so are and shall be utterly void and of none Effect, and in no wise to be put in Use or Execution.'[43] This law was, and is, the ancestor of all anti-monopoly laws – including the American Sherman Act, the European Union's competition laws and the laws of more than a hundred other nations.

The Statute of Monopolies would come to demonstrate the political potency of the anti-monopoly cause. For after James I died, Charles I again violated Parliament's monopoly ban and began handing out, or in some cases selling, state monopolies to raise money. The public rage at this and other abuses of

Parliamentary law eventually led to Charles being deposed and executed. As Hermann Levy would write, 'the fierce battle against monopolies during the reign of Charles I had left an almost inextinguishable mark on English economic sentiment.'[44] It would also influence British economists through the ages, as anti-monopoly sentiment 'passed from the mouths of the excited people into the classic writings of men like Adam Smith and David Ricardo'.[45]

The English origins of anti-monopoly law hold a few key lessons. Resistance to monopoly depends on a culture with room for popular and intellectual resistance. The new English laws depended on a vocal merchant class, jealous of what they regarded as a natural right to business, and protective of what would later be called their economic liberty. It was similar to the sentiments that would later inspire the Englishmen who began the American Revolution.

The second lesson is the importance of at least some separation of powers. At a time when most monarchs had near-absolute power, in sixteenth-century England power was dispersed and divided between the monarch, the aristocracy (the Lords), the common law courts and Parliament. This created room for the courts to intervene, and later for Parliament to act. And as I shall suggest throughout this book, the very existence of avenues for resistance can be all-important.

The English may have started things, but the idea soon spread, particularly to colonial America. For what not everyone remembers is that the American Revolution in some ways had been foreshadowed by the revolt against Charles I, and that abuse of monopoly by the Crown was one of its great sparks.

The American Anti-Monopoly Tradition

On the night of 16 December 1773, about sixty or so men, armed with axes, gathered in the Boston harbour, preparing to board three ships by force if necessary. The ships, the *Dartmouth*, *Eleanor* and *Beaver*, were already the scene of a stand-off. For more than two weeks, armed men, standing guard day and night, had prevented these ships from unloading their precious cargo, declaring in a pamphlet: 'The hour of destruction, of manly opposition to the machinations of tyranny, stares you in the face.'[46]

The source of the controversy and mutual threats of violence was monopoly tea. More precisely, the first shipments of tea belonging to the British East India Company, which, under the Tea Act of 1773, was given, by the King, a de facto monopoly on the export and sale of tea in the American colonies, provoking the anti-monopoly protests that would change history.

Earlier that day, local merchants and activists had appeared, not for the first time, before the royal governor of Massachusetts, and demanded that the ships go back to England. In New York and Philadelphia, fearing violence, the governors had already relented and sent similar ships back. But Thomas Hutchinson, the governor of Massachusetts, declared himself duty-bound to the King to allow the ships to unload,[47] and angrily declared that on the next day the ships would be unloaded, with the aid of British warships if necessary.

These declarations only had the effect of provoking the crowd into action. Inspired by a protestor dressed as a Mohawk Native American, some donned disguises. One of them, George R. T. Hewes, recounted, 'I immediately dressed myself in the costume of an Indian, equipped with a small hatchet, which I and my associates denominated the tomahawk. . . When I first appeared in the street after being thus disguised, I fell in with many who were dressed, equipped and painted as I was, and who fell in with me and marched in order to the place of our destination.'[48]

Thus attired and armed, the men boarded the ships *en masse*. In a coordinated operation, they demanded the keys to the holds, brought out the chests of tea, then broke them open with axes and dumped the chests overboard. There was no other violence, and no other damage done to the ships, but by the end of the night they had dumped 342 chests of tea into the harbour. As some of it was still floating in the harbour the next day, 'a number of small boats were manned by sailors and citizens, who rowed them into those parts of the harbour wherever the tea was visible, and by beating it with oars and paddles, so thoroughly drenched it, as to render its entire destruction inevitable.'[49]

As this suggests, the American anti-monopoly movement has historically been the world's most fervent, and in the times of its execution, the most intense in its remedies. In fact, this incident, known as the 'Boston Tea Party', led to British countermeasures against Boston, which, in their harshness, managed to spark what we now call the American Revolution.

More generally, the experience of British Crown monopolies yielded an anti-monopoly spirit that ran deep among the founding generation of Americans, including Thomas Jefferson, James Madison and others. Monopoly, they believed, was a form of abuse, an anathema to freedom, a violation of the natural rights of man. Jefferson felt the constitution should include a specific ban on monopolies.[50] He called for a declaration of rights: 'one which shall stipulate freedom of religion, freedom of the press, freedom of commerce against monopolies, trial by juries in all cases, no suspensions of the habeas corpus, no standing armies'.[51]

The American revolutionaries originally opposed the same monopolies as the English: government-imposed monopolies that they regarded as unjustified by any motive other than profit to the preferred. But the Americans would go much further than the English in the late nineteenth century, by passing the first laws designed to break purely private monopolies – more precisely, the corporate 'Trusts' of the Gilded Age. This gave birth to the 'antitrust' movement in the US, and while there is no one person who can be credited with starting the tradition, we can understand some of its ideas through one of its essential figures: the famed jurist and activist Louis Brandeis.

Brandeisian Thought

Louis Brandeis was born in 1856 in Louisville, Kentucky, the son of entrepreneurial immigrants from Prague.[52] As is probably true of most of us, but is particularly noticeable in Brandeis, his early years would have an important influence over his thinking. In particular, they gave him an indelible sense of what 'economic democracy' looks like.

The town of Louisville was, in Brandeis's youth, no world capital, nor the seat of any corporate empire, but nonetheless a flourishing regional centre, in a United States that was far more economically decentralized than it is today. It was, economically speaking, dominated not by a few large concerns but a multitude of small ones. It was a place that his father, an immigrant and farmer turned grain merchant, could come to and build a comfortable and dignified middle-class existence while running an ethical business. As a state historian put it, his father left behind the 'legacy of an incorruptible name and a first-class reputation for commercial sagacity and integrity'.

While the state still suffered the curse of agricultural slavery, Louisville was, at least to Brandeis, an 'idyllic' place, representing an 'economic democracy' – that is, a place of industrial freedom and openness to competition, yet with an economy that yielded adequate spoils for all. 'Louisville [during his youth]', writes Brandeis biographer Melvin Urofsky, 'seemed the quintessential democratic society, in which individuals. . . could do well by dint of their intelligence and perseverance. There were no large factories employing thousands of people, but rather many small endeavors – farms, stores, professional offices. People knew one another, their lives entwined in a strong sense of community.'[53]

After high school, Brandeis moved to Dresden, Germany, where he enrolled in the Annen-Realschule, and then to Boston, where he achieved famously high grades at Harvard Law School and developed a passion for canoeing and horseback riding.[54] Deciding to make his career in Boston, he built a distinguished legal practice and might have lived a completely uneventful life had he not become involved in politics due to his outrage at what was happening around him.

In the 1890s, by the time he reached his forties, the American economy was undergoing a major transformation – the 'monopoly movement'. A new form of corporation, the trust, had emerged to dominate the American economy. The best known was the Standard Oil Company, which had monopolized the oil refining industry in the 1870s, and invented the 'trust' as a form of legal organization. But this was just part of a broader trend: from 1897 to 1904, an estimated 4,227 manufacturing firms merged, leaving behind 257 corporations.[55] U.S. Steel, a firm even larger than Standard Oil, emerged from a massive merger of more than 220 American steel companies. There was also a Tobacco Trust, a Rubber Trust, a Nail Trust, a Film Trust and so on – one monopolist for every industry.

Brandeis experienced first-hand the trust movement's full march on the American economy as it acquired and demolished smaller businesses and independents. Many of Brandeis's clients were, like his father, small-business owners with whom he had a personal relationship. They became the targets of this economic transformation, which at its most extreme was like an industrial eugenics movement, viewing the small or traditional as unfit to survive industrial life. In his resistance to the trust movement Brandeis gained his identity and formulated the principles that are now his legacy.

Brandeis's views crystallized during a battle with a tributary of financier J. P. Morgan's railway empire. Among Morgan's many monopolization projects was the consolidation of the Northeastern rail and ferry transport infrastructure into one giant monopoly – the New Haven Railroad. Morgan sought to combine some 336 firms, including Boston's local railway line, the Boston and Maine, to forge a new system.[56] Outraged, Brandeis found his voice as the monopolization campaign's leading public opponent.

Brandeis, who was a business lawyer by trade, was hardly unsympathetic to the role business played in society. In fact, he was happy to praise good businesses that grew organically and built dignified operations beloved by customers and partners – the model provided by his own father.[57] But during his fight with Morgan and the New Haven Railroad, he developed a distrust, even a disgust, with the new class of corporate monopoly. For behind the happy talk and big promises, his own investigations suggested that the New Haven was building its monopoly by lying to investors, bribing politicians and professors, and buying off any opposition. 'Lying and sneaking are always bad, no matter what the ends,' said Brandeis later, privately. 'I don't care about punishing crime, but I am implacable in maintaining standards.'[58]

Over time, Brandeis came to believe that the New Haven represented the evils of what he called 'excessive bigness', for he watched it exterminate other businesses, mistreat workers, defraud investors and actually hide gross inefficiencies with size – all in the service of mere profits for bankers and speculators. As he put it, 'the evils of Bigness are something different from and additional to the evils of monopoly. A business may be too big to be efficient without being a monopoly; and it may be a monopoly and yet, so far as size is concerned, may be well within the limits of efficiency. Unfortunately, the so-called New Haven system suffers from both excessive bigness and from monopoly.'[59]

Brandeis came to fear that, as the corporations became large and powerful, they took on a life of their own and were increasingly insensitive to humanity's wants and fears. He put it this way in 1911: 'we are in a position, after the experience of the last twenty years, to state two things: In the first place, that a corporation may well be too large to be the most efficient instrument of production and distribution, and, in the second place, whether it has exceeded the point of greatest economic efficiency or not, it may be too large to be tolerated among the people who desire to be free.'[60]

As this quote suggests, what makes Brandeis's thought distinctive is his linking of economic structure to the very conditions of democracy and even the goals of human existence. If pre-industrial Louisville represented Brandeis's idea of what a democracy and economy might look like, he also had strong ideas of what a democratic economy was for.

For him, the very purpose of life was the development of character, and the development of self. The 'ideal' of democracy, he once said, should be 'the development of the individual for his own and the common good'.[61] He was in accord with the position taken by contemporary philosopher Wilhelm von Humboldt that 'the end of man, or that which is prescribed by the eternal or immutable dictates of reason. . . is the highest and most harmonious development of his powers to a complete and consistent whole.'[62]

That view had important implications for what the nation and its laws should look like. A worthy nation was one that served as a cauldron for character and self-development, one that 'compels us to strive for the development of the individual'.[63] Importantly, Brandeis didn't think that such personal growth was something that just happened: he believed that it required the right conditions. As he said: '[T]he "right to life" guaranteed by our Constitution' should be understood as 'the right to live, and not merely to exist. In order to live men must have the opportunity of developing their faculties; and they must live under conditions in which their faculties may develop naturally and healthfully.'[64]

A good country and a good economy, therefore, would be one that provided everybody with sufficient liberties and adequate support to live meaningful, fulfilling lives. He thought the American founders had understood this, that '[t]hey valued liberty both as an end, and as a means. They believed liberty to be the secret of happiness, and courage to be the secret of liberty.'[65] Hence, a worthy nation should protect men and women from any forces, public or private, that might stifle the opportunities for thriving and life. That would include, of course, government censorship and oppression – hence, the importance of free speech, free association and other liberties. But it also meant freedom from industrial domination, exploitation or so much economic insecurity that one could not really live without fear of unemployment and poverty. 'Men are not free,' he wrote, 'if dependent industrially on the arbitrary will of another.'[66] Economic security was a foundation on which one could really be free in a meaningful sense – hence, the importance of steady but not oppressive work, of education, time and space for leisure, parks, libraries and other institutions.

What Brandeis noticed is something we often ignore. It is one thing to speak of freedoms in the abstract, but for most people, a sense of autonomy is more influenced by private forces and economic structure than by government. For many if not most people, the conditions of work determine how much of life is lived – in such basic matters as the length of hours worked, the threat of being fired, harassed or mistreated by a boss, and for some jobs, questions as fundamental as personal safety or access to a toilet. Beyond work, our daily lives are shaped by rent, access to transport or groceries, and to healthcare. That is why Brandeis saw real freedom as freedom from both public and private oppression.

Brandeis saw an economy dominated by giant corporations as tending to inhumanity. He feared that working in a giant corporation might rob the American people of their character: 'far more serious even than the suppression of competition' was 'the suppression of industrial liberty, and indeed of manhood itself'. He grew to detest the growing American culture of overwork, whether self-inflicted, as in the private lawyer's case, or more menacingly, in the growing class of large firms who worked their employees past the limits of human endurance. As he once wrote of the oppressive conditions and long hours at the new industrial firms, they threatened to create 'a life so inhuman as to make our former Negro slavery infinitely preferable'.[67]

How did Brandeis's principles manifest themselves as economic policy? He took the view that government's highest role lay in the protection of human liberty and the provision of securities consistent with human thriving. That meant a commitment to civil liberties, like rights of free speech and privacy, protected by the courts. But it also meant a commitment to the protection of workers, and an open economy composed of smaller firms – along with measures to break or limit the power of monopolies.

On the positive side, Brandeis was an advocate of measures designed to make life worth living, or that would foster a republic of good character and true citizenry. That meant good public education, steady but not outrageous work hours, pensions for the aged and sufficient time for leisure and study. He wanted child labour to be banned, and the imposition of maximum work hours for others.[68] In short, he wanted the nation to be a place for citizens to thrive, not merely to survive.

The Ordoliberals

The Anglo-American world was the birthplace of the anti-monopoly tradition. But if it was later in coming, the Continental tradition was in many ways more advanced in its understanding of the relationship between private power and the state.

We have already discussed Germany's particular acceptance and celebration of monopolies and cartels in the decades before World War II. Yet so extreme was the German experience that by the 1930s it had yielded, in dissent, the anti-monopoly ideology known as Ordoliberalism, which would go on to transform post-war European thought.

German thinkers living in the 1930s and 1940s had first-hand experience of the maxim 'liberty, unprotected, destroys itself,' for they had seen markets become cartels and turn into monopolies. They had also witnessed the freedoms of democracy succumb to dictatorship. And living through Hitler's war, they could not fail to see the dangers of concentrated private firms serving the goals of the state.

The most outspoken Ordoliberal founders were Franz Böhm and Walter Eucken, both of the Freiburg school of economic thought that came out of Freiburg University. Böhm was born in 1895, grew up in southern Germany, and fought in the First World War. In the 1920s, he began work in the economic ministry of the Weimar Republic, and after the passing of a new cartel law in 1923, he worked in the cartel department. It was during the 1920s that the German economy began to fully monopolize through a process of industry-wide mergers, such as the merger that produced the German 'United Steel' syndicate. That period engendered in Böhm a lasting interest, even obsession, with private power and what he regarded as its corrupting effects on society.

In 1928, Böhm wrote 'Das Problem der privaten Macht, ein Beitrag zur Monopolfrage' (The Problem of Private Power, a Contribution to the Monopoly Question), which set out the basic proposition that economic governance was primarily a problem of managing private economic power. Böhm returned to academia in the 1930s, where he met Eucken and others. Eucken, born in 1891, was among those rare German conservatives who had recoiled when other conservatives became extremists and fascists. It was in reaction to the emerging Nazi economic order that Böhm and Eucken would set out the basic principles of what would later be called Ordoliberalism.

In 1936, Böhm, Eucken and a third co-author, Hans Großmann-Doerth, published the seminal Ordo Manifesto, originally entitled *Our Task*. Aggressive in its argument, it accused German economists, lawyers and philosophers of falling prey to 'relativism' and 'fatalism' when it came to accepting economic structures that were oppressive. They accused German thinkers of making the error of assuming that that which happens must be accepted, indeed celebrated, and thereby shedding any normative or critical perspective. This, they believed, made intellectuals mere puppets of the dictates of established economic powers.

'Fatalism and scepticism are always close to one another,' they wrote, for both 'make it seem pointless or foolish to pit oneself against the relentless course of events or to stand up for an idea'. The men blasted German intellectuals for confusing what *was* for what *should be.* '[We take] historicist fatalism for what it really is: a sign of weakness. . . Feeling their intellect to be insecure, they can no longer summon up the strength to tackle the job of shaping events and consequently, they retire to the role of observer[s].'[69]

In that same document, the Ordoliberals announced the importance of an 'economic constitution'. This was intended to link human freedom and economic policy in a manner not unlike Brandeis had set forth. And as Ordoliberalism developed, it focused on the fundamental question of developing a 'humane order for society', in the words of Eucken. This called for, in particular, a state that did not seek to eliminate the market or free economy, but rather to sustain its operation against the twin threats of public government power and concentrated private power.

Here is how Franz Böhm explained matters in 1947: 'Competition and anti-trust laws' are a 'fundamental and fateful issue precisely because they are concerned with harnessing this ordering power [of the market] and securing a full taste of this autonomy for free peoples'. He also echoed the premise that linked private concentration and war. 'Power concentration within the private market will always create potential for war. It matters not whether the command system is National Socialist, socialist or communist in character: what is decisive is the fact that each command system owns an extraordinarily extensive power apparatus which can be centrally deployed and mastered by a very small number of people, that individual positions of power are necessarily apportioned within oligopolistic procedures that can neither be overseen nor vetoed by the public. . .'[70]

Understanding the role of the state may help clarify Ordoliberalism. If believers in laissez-faire wanted the state to get out of the way, and if socialists and fascists believed in a state-commanded economy, the Ordoliberals were among the first to call for a 'third way'. They wanted a state that was strong enough to break private power, but not so strong as to take over society. They wanted the state to guarantee certain economic securities, but to leave the provisioning of most goods to the market process. In their work, the Ordoliberals often compared the ideal state to a good gardener, who, by cutting back on overgrowth, created the conditions for prosperity and human thriving.

If they wrote in different styles, there is much philosophical similarity between Brandeis and the Ordoliberals. What both feared was concentrated and unaccountable power: they did not care whether it was private or public. The Ordoliberals were more acutely sensitive to the problem of private power threatening the legitimate exercise of public power. The Ordoliberals believed that a lack of competition caused by cartels or monopolies distorted prices and production. But of equal importance to the Ordoliberals was the danger of a corruption of the government caused by private power. They believed the state was always in grave danger of capture by powerful private interests who would threaten the economic system and, ultimately, suspend democracy.

Writing as the Nazis were coming to power, this may have seemed a prescient warning. But Böhm and Eucken chose to rely on nineteenth-century examples, perhaps to avoid arrest. And yet, despite the fact their criticism of the Nazi regime was not explicit, Böhm and Eucken's advocacy of an open economy was obviously incompatible with the Nazi economic order. While not explicitly part of the resistance, both Böhm and Eucken were suspended from their positions in the late 1930s; Eucken was imprisoned for a period, and Böhm narrowly escaped probable execution after the failed plot against Hitler on 20 July 1944.

Fortunately they survived and became an important, if not pre-eminent intellectual influence over European economic policy through the 1950s and 1960s. Eventually, their cause was taken up by another man, Ludwig Erhard, who was among Germany's most important post-war leaders and himself a diehard Ordoliberal. It is to that period we now turn.

4

PEAK ANTI-MONOPOLY

It was during the post-war years of the 1950s and 1960s that strong anti-monopoly laws, based on the teachings of both Ordoliberal and American thought, became readily identifiable parts of functional democracy and political freedom. At this time, the laws reached the fullest extent of their power, influence and political support. Reflecting the mood, America's antitrust chief in the early 1960s, Lee Loevinger, would testify before Congress: 'The problems with which the antitrust laws are concerned – the problems of distribution of power within society – are second only to the questions of survival in the face of threats of nuclear weapons.'[71] As he said in a job interview with American attorney general Robert Kennedy, 'I believe in antitrust almost as a secular religion.'[72]

The United States has not always led by example, but when it came to post-war anti-concentration movement, it did just that. Wendell Berge, the head of the antitrust division, wrote: 'The United States will be one of the world's greatest powers in the molding of the postwar world. It can set an example.'[73] In 1945, as if to prove the point, the American judiciary affirmed a break-up of America's long-standing and primary aluminium monopolist, Alcoa.[74] The symbolism was hard to miss, for Alcoa had supplied the aluminium used to make the fighters, bombers, battleships and aircraft carriers which had helped America win the war. It was attacking not just German and Japanese firms, but its own monopolies as well.

The language of the Alcoa decision, authored by famed jurist Learned Hand, amounted to a stirring statement of the Brandeisian anti-monopoly creed featuring some of the most poetic phrases ever used in economic policy. Hand wrote of a law premised on 'the belief that great industrial consolidations are inherently undesirable, regardless of their economic results'. It was motivated by 'a desire to put an end to great aggregations of capital because of the helplessness of the individual before them'. As he summarized, 'It is possible, because of its indirect social or moral effect, to prefer a system of small producers, each dependent for his success upon his own skill and character, to one in which the great mass of those engaged must accept the direction of a few.'[75]

Meanwhile, in the American Congress, anti-monopoly fever ran hot, motivated by a widespread fear that corporation concentration and international cartels might threaten American democracy. As Senator Estes Kefauver put it, speaking on 12 December 1950:

> I think we must decide very quickly what sort of country we want to live in. . . I am not an alarmist, but the history of what has taken place in other nations where mergers and concentrations have placed economic control in the hands of a very few people is too clear to pass over easily. A point is eventually reached, and we are rapidly reaching that point in this country, where the public steps in to take over. The taking over always follows one or two methods and has one or two political results. It either results in a Fascist state or the nationalization of industries and thereafter a Socialist or Communist state.[76]

Concerns that excessive corporate concentration undermined democracy prompted Congress to strengthen the antitrust laws, in a new 'Anti-Merger Act'. Politically, the law was explicitly styled as a reaction to the German and Soviet examples. It passed by large majorities in 1950[77] and gave the government new tools to prevent the build-up of giant firms in advance, by controlling – or undoing – mergers. Instead of trying to break them up decades later, the idea was to prevent their formation in the first place. The Justice Department and the Federal Trade Commission now had a powerful new tool for controlling bigness.

Meanwhile, in Europe, interest in anti-monopoly laws spread after the war. In West Germany, the Allies imposed Rule 56, designed to eliminate all 'concentrations of economic power. . . which could be used by Germany as instruments of political or economic aggression'.[78] Other nations followed suit in the late 1940s and 1950s, including Britain, which passed a new monopoly law in 1948.[79]

The most influential of the new ideas came out of West Germany, owing much to the efforts of Ludwig Erhard, a committed Ordoliberal who was Minister of Economics for the first decade of West Germany's existence.[80] He sought to reopen the German economy by eliminating the lingering presence of the command economy implemented by the Nazis. And Erhard successfully pushed for West Germany's first self-imposed anti-monopoly law in 1957.[81]

It would be wrong to suggest that the Ordoliberals, or Ludwig Erhard, had universal support. The new German law was softer on cartels than the Ordoliberals would have wanted. Yet the enacting of such a law in the traditional home of the cartels was an achievement indeed. Meanwhile, vindicating Erhard's point that monopoly was not necessary for economic growth, West Germany would soon undergo an economic miracle that quadrupled the nation's production by 1958.[82]

In a fairly short time, West Germany would emerge from its devastation to take its place among the wealthiest nations in the world, while maintaining strong economic protections for its citizens, and also avoiding excessive inequality, or an economy centred on just a few cities or large monopolies. In many ways, post-war West Germany (before the return of neoliberalism) approached some of the ideals of Brandeis and Ordoliberalism, maintaining a decentralized economy without great inequality. And while the comparison may not be completely fair, over the same period West Germany greatly outperformed East Germany, which had kept and fortified the centralized, centrally planned economy that had been the previous German tradition.

Meanwhile, in Japan, the American occupation authority under General MacArthur began what were described as 'the most ambitious antitrust actions in history', culminating in the passage of a deconcentration law passed in 1947.[83] As one official warned, 'If the Zaibatsu are permitted to survive the conditions of defeat, they will continue to dominate Japan's postwar government. With the experience gained in this war, they will be able to prepare even more thoroughly for the next attempt to conquer East Asia by force of arms.'[84] Ultimately, the United States settled on a policy designed to create a 'foundation for a Japanese middle class and competitive capitalism'.[85]

The anti-*zaibatsu* programme started out strongly. Eighty-three firms were targeted by the American occupation, and by 1948 some forty-two companies were dissolved. Sixteen firms went out of existence, and twenty-six others formed 'heir' companies, often splitting into several smaller firms. The remaining forty-one firms were allowed to remain after diversifying their ownership interests.[86]

Among the major measures that the Americans undertook was forcing the ruling families to liquidate their banking holdings and sell their shares, thereby forcing the ownership of the *zaibatsu* out of the control of the old family dynasties. These two measures were almost certainly the most significant achievements of the post-war effort in Japan.

But the movement lost momentum, and break-up slowed considerably, particularly after the Korean War started, and as the United States sought to mould

Japan into a strong counterweight to Chinese and Soviet power. Some in the 1960s went as far as to suggest that the *zaibatsu* had managed to recreate themselves, and it is true that Japan's domestic anti-monopoly law would never become a paradigm of serious enforcement. It is also true that, in time, the Japanese state would return to the promotion of national champions, albeit in a less militaristic way. It is possible, moreover, that this state of affairs helps explain Japanese stagnation in the 1990s, as we discuss later.

Meanwhile, in Europe, as new competition laws spread across the continent, the event of greatest long-term significance was the introduction, in 1962, of the European Economic Community's (predecessor to the European Union) own competition law.[87] By 1964, the European Commission had achieved its first victory in the European Court of Justice, against a German company called Grundig that was attempting to create an exclusive franchise in France.[88] This began an enforcement tradition that would eventually become the world's most active and important.

The American enforcement of anti-monopoly laws reached its zenith in the 1960s. Armed with a new law, the Anti-Merger Act of 1950, an upcoming generation of trustbusters went to entirely new extremes in the interests of blocking any mergers that might threaten to increase industry concentration. Over the 1960s and 1970s, the Justice Department waged war on banks, grocery stores, shoe manufacturers and other entities. In its defence, the Justice Department maintained that Congress had enacted a broad anti-concentration mandate; it was concerned about 'creeping' concentration achieved 'not in a single acquisition but as the result of a series of acquisitions'.[89]

In short, in the United States, and to a lesser extent in Europe and Asia, the post-war era was characterized by bold efforts to tame capitalism in ways that hadn't been envisioned by the communists or socialists. This was a deliberate attempt to limit private power by offsetting it against public power. While controversial at the time, and still controversial today, it is notable that the peak of anti-monopoly enforcement coincided with a period of extraordinary gains in prosperity in the industrialized world, and also gains in wealth and income equality.

But resistance was building in the corporate sector and among financial conservatives, who argued that government was waging a war against capitalism itself. That resistance would erupt soon. But first, let us take a look at some of the big moments in anti-monopoly at its peak.

5

THE TECH EXPLOSION
OF THE 1980S AND 1990S

To chronicle all that the anti-monopoly laws did, or failed to do, around the world since the 1940s would not suit this, a small book on bigness. But the case can be made for anti-monopoly enforcement by focusing on what was arguably its greatest success – a series of American and European cases targeting the tech monopolies of the 1980s and 1990s. These are the storied and courageous campaigns against IBM, AT&T and Microsoft, some of the most powerful firms ever to have existed. Their break-up of these industries, as we now know, did not last. But in its time it created enormous economic opportunity and led to extraordinary innovation.

In 1970, what we now know as the global tech industry was unrecognizable. Computers were large and extraordinarily expensive machines; software was a service provided to those who bought computers.[90] The Internet was an obscure research project, and networking, such as it was, was the province of the phone company. Personal computers, software companies, not to mention the Internet, Web and smartphones were all, literally, science fiction.

In structure, monopoly ruled the day. The technology industry was dominated by a number of massive firms, closely allied with government, who were, typically, monopolists or national champions in their home country, or sometimes nationalized monopolies. In the United States, two firms dominated what we now call the tech industries. IBM, known as 'Big Blue', was the computer monopolist, thanks to its impressive System/360. But IBM was a mere midget compared to AT&T (the American Telephone and Telegraph Company), then the largest firm in the world, and the unquestioned monopolist of American communications.[91] The firm, a regulated monopolist, had a close relationship with the American government; among other things, it ran some of the military's nuclear laboratories in New Mexico,[92] and had deployed an intercontinental ballistic missile (ICBM) early-warning system across the north of Canada and Alaska.[93]

The United States was, at the time, not alone in favouring a 'national champion' model for its tech industries. Most advanced nations did: Britain had ICL and later British Telecom; Germany had Siemens, Telefunken and Deutsche Telekom; Italy had Olivetti. The Soviet Union had copied IBM's designs to create its own mainframes.

Meanwhile, Japan in the 1970s was seen as China is today: the rising power in the technology sector and the greatest challenger to the United States. This was due to its success in consumer electronics (Sony), its computer giants (NEC and Fujitsu) and its telecommunications monopoly (NTT). By the late 1970s and 1980s, there was wide speculation that Japan would surpass the United States as the world's leading technological power, and possibly the leading economic power.

The table was set for a classic international battle between national champions for global domination and control of the future. And with Europe and Japan gaining quickly on their American rivals, a basic logic suggested that the United States should do everything it could to support, nurture and help its greatest firms win the international battle.

Instead, the US – or at least the anti-monopoly parts of the US Government – broke from that script. Counter-intuitively, rather than helping IBM and AT&T, the federal government turned on them. In 1969 and 1974, the United States Justice Department filed antitrust lawsuits seeking the break-up of both companies. It would do the same thing in the 1990s against Microsoft, then America's leading tech firm and the most valuable company in the world.

According to the logic of national championship, the American move was irrational, stupid, even suicidal. Yet, it had its own, counter-intuitive logic. And as we shall see, it did much to make the United States the pre-eminent tech nation for years to come. These success stories, some of antitrust's greatest, warrant a closer look.

IBM

International Business Machines (IBM) was founded in 1911 as a manufacturer of machines for tabulating and data processing. By the 1960s, IBM had become the largest computer manufacturer in the world, the dominant manufacturer of general purpose, or 'mainframe', computers designed to be used by corporations, government agencies and other large institutions. By 1969, IBM had grown to 258,662 employees and $7.2 billion in annual revenues,[94] and its IBM System/360 was the world's most successful computer line. It was a proud company, even possessing its own anthem which went as follows:

EVER ONWARD – EVER ONWARD!
That's the spirit that has brought us fame!
We're big, but bigger we will be
We can't fail for all can see
That to serve humanity has been our aim![95]

Over the 1960s, there were long-standing complaints that IBM was maintaining its mainframe monopoly and scaring people away from supercomputers using anticompetitive, predatory and unethical practices. In 1969, after a long investigation, the US Justice Department charged IBM with 'monopoly maintenance'. According to the Justice Department, IBM had undertaken 'exclusionary and predatory conduct' to maintain its dominant position in 'general purpose digital computers'.[96]

For its violations, the government sought divestiture – that is, a full break-up of IBM into smaller parts. In that sense, the case was a classic example of the 'big case' tradition, whose goal was to restructure the industry entirely.

After some six years of discovery, the case finally went to trial in 1975. During the trial, IBM put up a vigorous defence, which it's thought may have cost as much as a billion dollars. The judge, David Edelstein, permitted the calling of a seemingly endless number of witnesses, for unlimited periods of time. One government witness testified for more than six months. Other trial days consisted of reading of depositions into the record. Many of these details were chronicled by legal writer Steven Brill, in a scathing piece that portrayed the entire trial as a fiasco, or, in his words, 'a farce of such mind-boggling proportions that any lawyer who now tries to find out about it. . . will be risking the same quicksand that devoured the lawyers involved in the case'.[97] The trial continued for an astonishing six years, but Ronald Reagan was elected as president, and the case was dropped.

But of more interest than the trial itself are the effects of the litigation on IBM's conduct and decision-making. For the fact that IBM had a 'policeman at the elbow' would have a profound effect on the development of the technology markets over the 1970s and 1980s. As William Kovacic put it, the 'case caused IBM to elevate the role of lawyers in shaping commercial strategy and seems to have led the firm to pull its competitive punches'.[98] But we can be more precise than that. The clearest impact of the attack on IBM was its contribution to the rise of an independent software industry. Nor is this development a small matter, given that the software industry today is worth $1.6 trillion in the US ($3 trillion globally) and employs 2.5 million people.[99]

In the 1960s, it was IBM's practice, and the practice of most other mainframe manufacturers, to 'bundle' software with hardware.[100] That is, software was sold as a service that was tied to the sale of its hardware – the IBM mainframe unit came with a contract by which IBM programmers wrote software customized to the needs of the customer. Any pre-packaged software was merely meant to illustrate for the customer what software might look like, like a model home for a prospective buyer.

As it became apparent that the Justice Department was planning on bringing an antitrust lawsuit, IBM's legal team began to conclude, as a legal matter, that the software-hardware bundle would be difficult to defend. IBM president and CEO Thomas Watson Jr. made the decision, late in 1968, to begin the process of unbundling IBM's software offerings from its hardware offerings.

On 23 June 1969 – sometimes called the software industry's 'independence day' – IBM, for the first time, made seventeen applications independently available for lease (though not yet for sale).[101] With the first release of pre-packaged software products by the world's dominant computer firm, the world of computing was never the same again. Richard Lilly, founder of a prominent 1970s software firm, said in 1989, 'It created the industry we're in.'[102]

Estimating the economic importance of this development – and the contribution of IBM's unbundling – is not easy, if only because the transformation was so far-reaching. An important fact, however, is that the impact was not felt all at once. Hardware continued to be more important than software, and even into the 1980s, the software industry remained relatively small. One economic analysis suggests that 'in 1987, the receipts of U.S. software programming service companies (SIC 7371) were $14.2 billion, the receipts for computer integrated systems design (SIC 7373) were $7.1 billion, and the receipts from pre-packaged software (SIC 7372) sales were $5.9 billion.'[103] Other developments, like the triumph of the personal computer over all aspects of business computing, were yet to come. Yet by the 2010s, providers of software, even narrowly construed, were responsible for trillions of dollars in global revenue.

The IBM antitrust lawsuit was also key to another epochal change – the development of the personal computer industry. By the 1970s, a number of researchers, particularly those associated with Xerox's Palo Alto research centre, and hobbyists like Steve Jobs and Steve Wozniak, had come up with the idea of a 'personal' computer – something different to the giant machines owned by corporations and governments. By the late 1970s, a group of small, hobbyist firms, including Apple, and forgotten competitors like

Sinclair, Commodore, Acorn and Tandy, had ignited the market with the successful launch of the first mass-market personal computers. The firms proved that personal computers could be produced for less than $2,000, and that there was a market for them.[104]

Fledgling industries are often taken over or destroyed by monopolists – the so-called 'Kronos effect', named after the Greek titan who ate his own children. Many were concerned that the personal computer industry would not survive the inevitable onslaught of IBM, still by far the dominant manufacturer of computers.

In 1981, IBM entered the market, but with hindsight the influence of the policeman at the elbow is clear. The first IBM PC, however, was an extraordinarily radical break from IBM's traditional 'closed' system. The IBM PC team selected a hard drive manufactured by Seagate, a printer made by Epson, a processor made by Intel, instead of its own processors, and, most importantly over the long term, an operating system provided by Micro-Soft, then a small start-up, headed by a Bill Gates who was just twenty-five at the time and lacking a college degree.[105] In the end, when the PC came out, only the keyboard, screen, motherboard and hardware BIOS (Basic Input Output System) were actually produced by IBM's internal divisions.

Meanwhile, when IBM contracted with Microsoft to provide the main operating system for the computer, it neither bought the rights to the software nor even required an exclusive licence. The agreement was, instead, non-exclusive, leaving Microsoft free to sell its MS-DOS to other computer manufacturers as well.

In most histories of the computer industry, this is taken as a colossal blunder and a sign of Bill Gates's genius. But these histories forget that IBM was negotiating with one hand tied behind its back. Joseph Porac notes that 'a reluctance to overcontrol small companies that could become potential competitors [was an] offshoot of the company's antitrust phobia. Signing a nonexclusive contract with Microsoft that was clearly to Microsoft's benefit was one way of avoiding any future claim that IBM was dominating the personal computer market.'[106]

In the 1990s, reporters first revealed that, in fact, IBM was offered various opportunities to buy Microsoft or its software. In 1980, according to the *Wall Street Journal*, Microsoft offered to let IBM buy its operating system outright, an opportunity that IBM declined – Charles Ferguson and Charles Morris wrote that 'because of the still-pending antitrust action, IBM was wary of owning operating system software for fear of suits from software writers' for 'IBM was extremely sensitive to even the appearance of having an unfair advantage over a small supplier.'[107]

The bottom line is that IBM entered the PC market in a manner that can only be described as strangely and exceptionally stimulating to competition and, indeed, in a manner that breathed life into firms and nascent industries. In fact, the level of competition ended up being much greater than IBM could possibly have anticipated. The most important consequence was the fostering of a whole range of new and independent industries: an industry for hard drives and other forms of storage, another for processors and memory, and, of course, the market for personal computer software. This is what has made computing equipment affordable – at some level, it is a big part of the personal computer revolution.

Here was the law at its best – challenging the powerful, and changing the incentives of firms and the structure of the market in a way that creates new industries and opportunities. But IBM was really a warm-up for the attack on America's great telecommunications monopolist, AT&T.

The Break-Up of the World's Largest Firm

In 1974, AT&T was the largest firm on the planet, the employer of over a million people, and the uncontested holder of a monopoly that had, by then, lasted a full six decades. Created by J. P. Morgan, it was the most important and powerful incarnation of the corporatist vision; the colossus restrained, its activities carefully regulated by the Federal Communications Commission, under the banner of 'regulated monopoly'.

Life, in other words, was fine for the world's greatest blue whale, until 1974, when the White House announced a surprising change in policy. 'Unless the would-be monopolist [AT&T] or the public can demonstrate special public policy considerations that justify monopoly, it should not be permitted.'[108] Later that same year, the Justice Department filed suits against AT&T, producing the largest and perhaps most consequential case in the entire history of the competition laws. This resulted in the last massive break-up, and arguably the most successful in terms of its effect on the American economy, of the post-war era.

We should be a little more precise: AT&T was not the mere holder of a monopoly, but multiple monopolies – six or seven, depending on how one counts – making it the quintessential 'super monopolist'. At its height the firm controlled local telephone services, long-distance services, the physical telephones, all other attachments, business telephone services and markets just coming into existence, including 'online' services.

Nowadays, even dominant firms at least pay lip service to the importance of competition. Not so with AT&T, which even at the time was unusual in its ideological dedication to monopoly rule. That was a tone set by AT&T's first true ruler, Theodore Vail, who had made his reasoning moralistic, arguing that competition was giving American business a bad name: 'The vicious acts associated with aggressive competition are responsible for much, if not all, of the present antagonism in the public mind to business, particularly to large business.'[109]

Over the years, AT&T had not been content to be merely the neighbourhood telephone monopolist. No, AT&T was the jealous God of telecommunications, brooking no rivals, accepting no sharing, and swallowing any children with even the remotest chance of unseating Kronos. As it insisted to the Federal Communications Commission (FCC) in 1968, competition was inconsistent with its very mission of running a phone system: hence, the Bell companies 'must have absolute control over the quality, installation, and maintenance of all parts of the [telephone] system in order effectively to carry out that responsibility'.[110] Much trouble came from this deep aversion to competition. Almost as if unable to help itself, it did everything it could to kill MCI, a tiny rival that used microwave towers to offer cheaper long-distance services, along with trying to block anyone daring to offer a service competing with

Bell's telephones.[111] Over the 1970s, the firm became even more aggressive in its attacks on competitors, despite the ongoing investigation. Its seventh decade would be its last.

One of the real triggers was political, even constitutional. The Justice Department felt that AT&T had become a rival to the state, showing itself resistant to government control. Faced with regulation by government, including the ancestor of net neutrality rules, Bell had managed to subvert or undermine many of these policies. It was the idea of a monopolist that considered itself above government control that compelled the Justice Department to action.

The AT&T litigation lasted a decade, but created no great court decision. In the early 1980s, during the Reagan administration, AT&T agreed to a dramatic break-up. It was divided into eight smaller firms and placed under several restraints as to what business they might conduct.[112] Each of the new firms would be obliged to accept connections from any long-distance company (not just their former parent), and all were explicitly shut out of new markets such as online services and cable.

As the last great American break-up, it is worth examining what consequences it had. It unquestionably created chaos over the short term. Though some economists point to lower prices in the wake of the dissolution, the real impact was different and far more important. It became apparent, in retrospect, just how much innovation the Bell system monopoly had been holding back. Out of the carcass of AT&T emerged entirely new types of industries unimagined or unimaginable during its reign.

For example, a new freedom to sell things to consumers yielded not only the answering machine, but the modem, allowing a home computer to speak with a network. That, in turn, made feasible an industry of online service providers like AOL or CompuServe, which themselves spawned Internet service providers that were accessible from home, producing the successive Silicon Valley booms.

Obviously, not everything that happened over the 1980s and 1990s can be attributed to the AT&T break-up. Yet under the Bell system, its control was so pervasive that many of these businesses would have been impossible to start. That – the sparking of the Internet revolution – is surely among the anti-monopoly law's greatest achievements.

Japan Under Central Planning

Over the same period in the 1970s, the Japanese tech industry was clearly challenging the United States for dominance. At the time, Japan was a hotbed of world-changing innovations. Firms like Sony, Panasonic and Toshiba met their first success by creating cheaper copies of American mainstays, like the television and the radio. But some – especially Sony – had shown a magic touch for introducing twists on existing products, the best example of which was the Walkman, an easily portable cassette player that attached to one's belt. As the first technological device that allowed a person to walk down the street encased in their own musical reality, the Walkman quickly became a craze.

Soon Japan was also beating the Americans at the 'next thing': the new video games appearing in video arcades around the world. If a game named *Pong*, written by Californian firm Atari, got things started, Japanese companies soon came to dominate the market. The first real blockbuster was a Japanese game originally entitled *Supēsu Inbēdā*,, which became more widely known as *Space Invaders*. The game asked the player to shoot down an incoming army of aliens, and created a worldwide sensation. And *Space Invaders* was just the first of a series of Japanese blockbusters, including '*Pakku Man*' (*Pac-Man*), *Donkey Kong* and others.

But Japan's success wasn't to last. Flush with a sense that it was winning, the Japanese government, in the early 1980s, made a critical error. It bet too heavily on centralized technological planning, backed by the government's Ministry of International Trade and Industry, which many believed could do no wrong. A key example was Japan's master plan for the domination of global camputing. It must certainly have sounded like a good idea at the time. Japan consulted with experts who confidently predicted that larger and faster computers were the future, and that Japan was in a race with the United States and Europe to be the first to build a massively parallel supercomputer. The key to winning the race would be the 'Fifth Generation' computing project, a giant collaboration between the Japanese government and its greatest computer giants. As a 1984 article explained, 'the Japanese are planning the miracle product. It will come not from their mines, their wells, their fields, or even their seas. It comes instead from their brains. . . They're going to give the world the next generation – Fifth Generation – of computers, and those machines are going to be intelligent.'[113]

But it turned out that Japan had not so much bet on the wrong horse, but that it was running the wrong race. The supposedly safe bet on supercomputing turned out to be a total failure, missing, as it did, the importance of less grandiose innovations, such as personal computers, the graphical user interface on the Apple Macintosh, and the computer networking we now call the Internet. The project was an abject failure that permanently damaged the Japanese computer industry. 'Critics pronounced it a complete failure, while supporters were confined to citing collateral benefits such as researcher training.'[114]

Meanwhile, as the United States was breaking up AT&T, the Japanese government declined to do anything so bold. Its 'break-up' of Nippon Telegraph and Telephone (NTT) in the 1990s allowed the company to maintain control of the constitutive parts.[115] Consequently, Japan never developed a significant software industry, but instead, following the model of NEC and NTT, maintained a focus on hardware-centred, integrated systems. There was no 'online industry' and no boom of start-ups.

Japan wasn't the only major nation to make this mistake. The Europeans, while sometimes vigorous in their enforcement of competition, were rarely willing to take on the favoured state monopolies of individual countries. The largest nations, sticking with corporatism, left their telecom monopolists intact, and found their computing industries perpetually relegated to the sidelines. The exception was the Scandinavians, out on the periphery of Europe, who managed to nurture and develop an independent software industry.

Finally, Japan seemed to leap ahead of the United

States in the 1990s, with its leading-edge cellphones, based on Japan's great ability to design hardware. But the mobile industry's offerings remained, mainly, those of a duopoly of phone companies.[116] A start-up culture did not develop, and Japan's brief lead soon disappeared. And because Japan never broke the power of its telephone monopoly, independent telecommunications and Internet firms never really grew. By the early 2000s, the United States had leapt far ahead. There is, after all, only so much you can do when your innovations need to be engineered so as not to disturb the mother ship.

By the 1990s, Japan, now late to both software and personal computing, began to lag behind the United States. Limited by NTT, it then proceeded to miss the Internet revolution – not a single Japanese firm of note emerged in the 1990s or early 2000s. Looking back, Japan's tech sector largely missed out on the software, personal computer and Internet revolutions. It never really recovered.

In some ways, Japan ignored the real lessons of its success in computer electronics and video games. For its success in those areas had been the province of smaller, scrappier firms like Sony, Toshiba, Taito and Nintendo. Yet Japan somehow thought that hulking giants like its own NTT or NEC would command the future. It was wrong.

History is complicated, and there is more than one reason that Japan lost the tech race of the 1980s and 1990s. But there are good reasons to believe that getting IBM and AT&T out of the way at a time when new ideas were ripe to flourish played a major role in the return of the United States to tech dominance.

Before the American anti-monopoly tradition fell into its current hibernation, it would yield one final case of lasting importance. In the 1990s, the enforcers filed suit against the richest man on earth and the most valuable company: Bill Gates and his Microsoft Corporation.

Microsoft

The Microsoft of the 1990s was a different sort of creature to the gentle giant it would later become. It was an aggressive, cunning and often abusive machine, ruthlessly dispatching its various rivals. Its founder and leader, Bill Gates, before he became a philanthropist, was the archetype of the evil nerd, a brilliant strategist who, while rarely holding the better technologies, nonetheless managed to consistently beat and outplay the firms that did.

Gates had an undeniable gift for foreseeing the future as well as the ambition to try to control it. By 1995, he'd noticed that this whole 'Internet' thing might threaten Microsoft's dominance over much of the computing industries. As he pointed out in a secret memo entitled 'The Internet Tidal Wave', it was very possible that people might come to think of the Web as more important than the applications running on their computers, and of the browser as more important than their operating systems.[117] He was right: Microsoft's two main monopolies were endangered.

Gates also had an acute sensitivity to where the points of control in his industry were to be found: he quickly seized on the Web browser as the key to the future. At the time, the leading browser, Navigator, was the product of a darling little company named Netscape. It was the first browser with truly mass popularity. To control the browser, Gates realized, would be to gain control over the future of the Web, and, as it later became clear, pretty much the future of the world.

It was an acute insight, but not an unfamiliar one, because it was actually a replica of the manoeuvre that Gates had built his entire fortune on. From the beginning, Microsoft had proven the mantra that good artists copy but great artists steal. Its first operating system (PC-DOS) was modelled on CP/M, an earlier operating system; and at its core was not Microsoft's own code, but a program named 86-DOS written by another firm.[118] In the 1990s, Microsoft Windows was an obvious copy of the Apple Macintosh operating system; Microsoft Word and Excel were copies of WordPerfect and Lotus 1-2-3, respectively. In no instance were Microsoft's products the first or better in a clear way – instead, they were always bundled with something else you wanted. Microsoft's products never won by choice, but rather, by the sense that there was no real choice, and this was Gates's real genius.

By the late 1990s, Microsoft had unleashed its signature strategy against Netscape. Explorer, Microsoft's copy of Navigator, was suddenly everywhere and Navigator was nowhere. This was no accident, but rather the by-product of coercive deals foisted on the entire industry by Microsoft.[119] In a few short years, Netscape was bankrupt, and Microsoft had added a new monopoly to its collection.

In our times, with minimal antitrust enforcement, Microsoft would have been in a perfect position to control the future of the Internet, just as Gates had planned. In the early 2000s, small firms like Google, Facebook, Amazon and others were all dependent on the Web browser, over which Microsoft now had a monopoly. In fact, I once asked Gates what would have happened in the absence of government action.

He said that he thought Microsoft had been perfectly positioned to control mobile operating systems now dominated by Apple and Google, but 'got distracted'. (To his credit, Gates suggested that the case led him to leave Microsoft for a career in philanthropy, and 'that's been a good thing.')

If you think Big Tech is today too powerful and too concentrated, imagine a world dominated, not by five or six large companies, but by one super-monopoly that dominated operating systems, desktop and mobile, search, and perhaps social networking as well. That might have been our future, had Microsoft not run into Joel Klein, President Bill Clinton's second head of antitrust at the Justice Department, and the European Commission. Many thought Klein was a mild-mannered laissez-faire kind of guy. But he surprised everyone with his aggressive prosecution of the Microsoft monopoly. 'Where I think there is a case, I want to litigate,' he told the *Washington Post*. 'I'm not looking for seven cents on the dollar, or something like that.'[120]

Meanwhile, in Europe, the EU's Commissioner for Competition, Mario Monti, nicknamed 'Super Mario', would also prove immune to Microsoft's charm. The EU officially filed suit in 2004, and the Europeans would end up torturing the company for far longer than the Americans.

Yet even though Microsoft, which had a market share of over 90 per cent, was engaged in the destruction of a small company with the goal of acquiring a new monopoly in a new market, many attacked Klein for bringing suit. Tech markets were too complicated or 'fast-moving' for the law to catch up. The government doesn't understand tech. It would kill the goose laying the golden eggs.

But the facts, as they came out, strongly favoured the Justice Department. Microsoft's motives were made clear by its internal memoranda; and Microsoft had great difficulty coming up with anything but the most pretextual reasons for the tactics it employed against Netscape. Bill Gates endured a brutal and lengthy deposition, which revealed a far darker side to the man than his various hagiographies had depicted.

The Justice Department won in district court, and then won on appeal, and seemed to be cruising towards another big break-up. In Europe, similarly, the Commission determined that Microsoft had abused its dominance. Big case antitrust, it seemed, was alive and well. But it was around this time that George W. Bush won the 2000 presidential election by a small and contested margin of the Florida vote. Not too long thereafter, his Justice Department settled the Microsoft litigation without breaking up the firm. It was a sign of things to come; for with that, the American anti-monopoly programme, once the world's strongest and most vigorous, entered a deep freeze from which it has yet to properly emerge.

6

NEOLIBERALISM'S TRIUMPH

Intellectual movements, like waves, do not move in the same direction at the same time. Instead, they go in their own directions, sometimes making each other stronger, but sometimes cancelling each other out.

So it was in the 1990s, when it came to the thinking behind corporate concentration and global monopoly. On the one hand, it might have been reckoned to be the greatest hour for competition laws, as they spread to nearly all of the world's countries, and as Europe reinforced its legislation. The basic premise that completely unfettered capitalism yielded bad outcomes had been broadly accepted, and nearly every developed nation enacted its own anti-monopoly laws, most modelled on European and American exemplars.

Yet strangely enough, the law itself was increasingly defanged and diluted even as it reached more places. To understand this, we must understand an ideological transformation under way – the victory of neoliberalism over Ordoliberalism.

The ideology of neoliberalism had been a competitor to Ordoliberalism, the latter being the ideology that inspired Germany's adoption of an anti-monopoly law and ultimately the creation of a European competition law. Both Ordoliberalism and neoliberalism believed in the importance of human liberty in matters of politics and economics, and of a free market – the liberty for men and women to pursue their trades. But the key difference was this: the Ordoliberals believed, as we said earlier, that liberty, unprotected, destroys itself. In other words, an open economy without protector for competition will become a monopoly; and a democracy without protections will become a dictatorship. The Ordoliberals watched both of these things happen in Germany over the 1930s. They therefore believed in interventions by the state to protect human liberty, both in matters of economics and civil liberties.

In contrast, neoliberalism was opposed to almost all forms of state intervention in the economy, though this hadn't always been the case. In its earlier forms at least, neoliberalism had an anti-monopoly streak.

As promoted by Friedrich Hayek, it was meant to be a means for preventing the rise of a totalitarian state, and was, as such, also anti-monopolistic.[121] Like the Ordoliberals and the American government, Hayek recognized the grave danger that arose from the combination of monopoly and state power.

Yet as neoliberal, anti-government ideologies gained strength over the 1970s and 1980s, something surprising happened. The movement would, rather astonishingly, shed its resistance to monopoly; indeed, it became tolerant of monopoly, even of government-supported monopoly. The latter might seem so stark a refutation of its origins as to be unbelievable. How this came to pass, beginning in the United States, the very country that had invented the anti-monopoly laws themselves, is the story we now tell.

In America: Chicago and Harvard Triumphant

Aaron Director, the father of the neo-conservative Chicago School of antitrust, was a mysterious figure who left behind few written works, but whose students were many and whose intellectual influence over late-twentieth-century legal thought is matched by few. Born in the Russian Empire, he emigrated with his parents and grew up in Portland, Oregon. Attending Yale University as an undergraduate in the 1920s, he became enamoured with socialism, so much so that he and his friend Mark Rothko, the artist, together published a leftist-socialist newsletter.

But at some point in the 1930s, Director lost his fascination with socialist thought. He studied labour economics at the University of Chicago, and by the end of the 1940s, despite the lack of a law degree or a PhD in economics, he found work co-teaching antitrust law at the University of Chicago.[122]

Director's lack of extensive graduate education in economics might actually have helped him, for he began his studies during a period in which economists on the left and right rejected the idea that markets worked well by themselves. As Donald Dewey writes, 'not a single American-trained economist of any prominence questioned the desirability of antitrust in the interwar years.'[123]

Liberal economists tended to support antitrust as a counter to the dominating force of big business. Conservatives feared 'a road to serfdom', in Friedrich Hayek's phrase, resulting from central planning accomplished through a union of monopolies and the state. Some thought of monopolies as a threat to economic freedom by themselves; others feared that private monopolies provided an excuse for nationalization or at least extensive regulation. Here is conservative economist George Stigler, writing in 1952: 'The dissolution of big businesses is necessary to increase the support for a private, competitive enterprise economy, and to reverse the drift toward government control.'[124]

Director's big idea was brilliant in its simplicity. Working with classic price theories, which at the time had been discarded as unrealistic by most of the economics profession, he attacked American law as counterproductive in terms of 'consumer welfare'. By this he meant the measure of whether the economic prospects of the consumer were enhanced in a measurable way: that is, by lower prices.

Director feared that a Brandeisian programme of breaking up monopolies or protecting competition might simply protect weaker, less efficient companies from more efficient firms that might lower prices for consumers. For Director, if one big company threatened to put every other retailer out of business, the only thing that the law should care about is whether prices for consumers might go up or down. Any other consideration was completely illegitimate. Only prices mattered.

At the time, these views put Director and his 'Chicago School' followers in what some called the lunatic fringe.[125] To become influential, Director needed a lawyer. Fortunately, he would find his advocate in the greatest and most loyal of his students, a man named Robert Bork.

Robert Bork is famous to Americans for being the man that the American Senate blocked from the Supreme Court in the 1980s due to the extremity of his right-wing views. A veteran of the Nixon administration, he was apparently always drawn to extremes: sometime in his youth, he surprised his parents and classmates by declaring himself a socialist and remained loyal to that cause throughout college. Bork originally wanted to be a journalist and writer, in the model of Ernest Hemingway. Like Hemingway, he liked to box, and he also made an effort to join the Marines in 1944, though he saw no combat.

By the time he entered law school in the 1950s, Bork was no longer enamoured with socialism – he considered himself a New Deal liberal instead. And so things were, and might have stayed, had not Bork taken a class from Aaron Director.

During that semester, Bork underwent what he later called a 'religious conversion'.[126] As Bork later recalled, 'Aaron gradually destroyed my dreams of socialism with price theory.'[127] He was convinced that Director was right, and that, in particular, the antitrust law was a misguided, if not doomed, project. He would become a self-described 'janissary', or loyal soldier, for Director.[128] As the switch from socialism to free-market libertarianism suggests, Bork dwelt in the poles, preferring strong positions, which he stated with eloquence and confidence. And unlike Director or other Chicago School economists, he was a first-rate lawyer, with a gift for writing persuasively.

Bork's contribution was to take Director's ideas and argue they weren't merely Director's inventions, but the actual intent of the laws all along. Working with his Chicago allies, he then created a fully formed alternative reality in which the anti-monopoly laws were not actually anti-monopoly, but only concerned with prices. In the 1960s, when he first presented the thesis, it was considered absurd and even insane. But within twenty years he'd manage to elevate his ideas to the law of the United States.

Bork promulgated the Director gospel: the only goal of the American laws was lower prices, despite mountains of evidence to the contrary. Absolute certainty in the face of much contradictory evidence was classic Bork. And he succeeded because he managed skilfully to tie his Chicago School theories to another, very powerful locomotive that was just beginning its run in the late 1960s in the United States – the rise of a conservative movement anchored by figures like Ronald Reagan, demanding that government do more to regulate morality, and less to regulate business.

Bork appealed to the broad middle by managing to tie the culture war to his approach. He presented the alternatives as a disreputable undertaking, the indulgence of liberals, somehow degenerate and debauched. Price-driven economic analysis, as portrayed by Bork, was righteous and self-restrained. As such, Bork managed to embed a new kind of moralism into methods of interpreting the law.

The truth is that lawyers and judges are anxious people, unusually desperate for respectability. Bork and his allies offered a way to decide cases that offered the appearance of rigour and even scientific certainty. Hence, the Chicago School succeeded because over the 1970s and 1980s it managed to conquer those in the middle who would later be known as neoliberals. By the 1970s, if Chicago represented a fringe of intellectual thought, the centre was occupied by the so-called Harvard School and, in particular, two professors, Donald Turner and Phillip Areeda, who wrote what remains the most influential guide to American competition and monopoly law.

Lawyers have their own culture and, at some level, the Chicago School and the neoliberals won the culture war by convincing a vast middle comprised of practising lawyers and judges seeking that respectability offered by price-driven economics. Bit by bit, the Chicago critique reached deeper into American law until it touched the core question of monopoly. And here, breaking with the fundament of its tradition, the law underwent a truly radical change, and suddenly became extraordinarily tolerant of the monopolist's conduct.

The contemporary monopolist, so the Chicagoans said, had been gravely misunderstood. He was not the threatening brute feared by previous generations, but a well-meaning and timid creature, almost a gentle giant, whose every action was well intentioned and who lived in constant fear of new competitors. Even if he had already killed his actual competitors, he was nonetheless restrained by just the thought of them. For that reason, he would not dare raise prices or destroy his rivals. This theory was deployed to defend AT&T, which was among the most entrenched monopolists in American history, while also apparently so afraid of potential competition that any wrongdoing was unthinkable.

When it came to the monopolist's abuses, there had just been a great misunderstanding. Everything was actually being done for the best and happiest of reasons. A cascade of Chicago School papers, based purely on pricing theory and ignoring any strategic considerations (let alone evidence), suggested that the monopolist had little to gain from these practices, and so must presumably be using them to make their operations more efficient. After all, one acolyte had said, one must always presume that 'the existing structure is the efficient structure'.[129]

Jumping from theory to reality in a novel way, the Chicago School then asserted that that which did not exist in theory likely did not exist in practice. Robbing banks is economically irrational, given security guards and meagre returns; ergo, bank robbing does not happen; ergo, there is no need for the criminal law. Exaggerated only slightly, this premise has been at the core of Bork–Chicago thinking for more than thirty years.

To be sure, these ideas ran into a speed bump during the years in which Bill Clinton was president and Microsoft was nearly broken up. But those years were, in the end, just a delay, for during the Bush years, the anti-monopoly provisions of the Sherman Act went into a deep freeze from which they have never really recovered. After pausing briefly to settle the Microsoft case, the Bush Justice Department completely ceased anti-monopoly enforcement, with a grand total of zero anti-monopoly cases over a period of eight years, and did not block any major mergers.

The Chicago virus would soon infect Europe as well. The European competition law was, as we've seen, founded on the Ordoliberal premise that a competitive market economy served human freedom and helped serve as a buffer against the rise of dictatorship. But over the 1990s, the European Commission began to embrace an interpretation of its own law that also elevated 'consumer welfare' as a goal to be considered above any other.

It was in 1997 that Europe, for the first time, began using Robert Bork's language, suggesting, in a green paper, that 'consumer welfare' and 'lower prices' were the goal of Commission action.[130] In 2005, as part of a modernization initiative, the Commission broadly declared that 'enhancing consumer welfare' and 'ensuring an efficient allocation of resources' were the ultimate aims of the Commission's work.[131]

The Ordoliberals of the 1930s would have agreed that keeping prices lower for consumers was important and beneficial. But they would have rejected the idea that this on its own could form the reason for preventing the concentration of private power. That would have struck them as absurd, for they were concerned with real questions of human freedom and had seen the danger posed by an over-concentrated economy. They would have feared the concentration of private power as a threat to the individual.

The changes made by the European Commission in 2005, like the technocratic moderates in the United States, was well intentioned. As in the United States, the goal was largely technocratic and in pursuit of 'rigour'. After all, ideas like 'private power' and 'economic freedom' are hard to quantify. A generation of bureaucrats wanted the sense of scientific certainty. With the new standard, Europe could pay economists to perform calculations and declare action either warranted or unwarranted. The great promise was making the law precise, scientific and predictable.

But in that mission, the project failed, both in the United States and Europe. It turns out that many of the things that matter – dynamic competition, destruction of competition, innovation, product quality, and even prices – are often unmeasurable. The quest for rigour just led to inaction. The only thing that became predictable was systematic under-enforcement. Companies soon learned that, with the right lawyers and economic experts, the new standard could be massaged; and that, at worst, a few conditions could be agreed to, and the government would go away.

Among the many problems created by the widespread adoption of a consumer welfare standard, there is one that stands out. That is the allowance of consolidations of industry through successive mergers that would have been shocking to other generations – consolidations that the Ordoliberals and Brandeisians would have been unable to believe. In the space of just over one generation, aided by the globalization of commerce and finance, we have seen consolidations around the world, both national and international, that beggar belief and make a mockery of the ideals of competition and economic freedom, while exerting intense pressure on small and medium producers and employees. Such is the reality of the curse of bigness in our time.

7

THE PROBLEM OF GLOBAL MONOPOLY

The sale of upscale glasses and sunglasses may seem, to the casual buyer, a highly competitive business. Walk into an eyewear store like Sunglass Hut and you'll see sunglasses from Armani, Ray-Ban, Tiffany, DKNY, Burberry and dozens of other brands. There are different styles for men and women, polarized lenses, sports lenses and so on.

But what looks like a healthy market is a grand deception. For what you may not realize is that each of these brands is owned by, or exclusively licensed by, just one company, which, in all likelihood, also owns the store you are in. The firm is Luxottica – the world's global eyeglass monopolist.

You may also not realize just what kind of profit margin is being earned on glasses; it is extraordinary even by retail standards, sometimes exceeding 5,000 per cent of cost. Over the past twenty years, even as Chinese manufacturing has made glasses cheaper, and technological advances have made the manufacturing of glasses more efficient, the prices keep going up instead of down, a perversion of the idea that efficiency helps consumers.

If you live in Europe, the United States or South America, you probably paid somewhere between US$125 and US$400, maybe as much as $800 for prescription lenses. Yet good quality frames can now be made for between $4 and $8, with the highest quality costing about $15. Lenses, meanwhile, of excellent quality, cost about $1.25 to make. In other words, it is not uncommon to pay over $200 for sunglasses that may cost $8 to manufacture. Or $400 for prescription glasses that cost $16.[132] This is the economy in which we live.

When prices keep going up, even as costs go down, something is seriously wrong. This is a symptom of the growing problem of global monopoly – an unexpected side effect of globalization with little to say in its favour. What Luxottica does is take advantage of a global supply chain, effectively uniting Chinese manufacturing with prized European and American brands and selling them in its worldwide retail spaces. This global supply chain has made lower costs possible – one of the promises of globalism – but instead of passing on the savings to consumers or perhaps workers, businesses keep them for themselves by maintaining high prices and even raising prices to whatever the market will bear. This is a global problem, typified by Luxottica; moreover, it's a problem for which the world presently lacks a solution.

Luxottica's own story is one of global consolidation. Founded in Italy in 1961, it began its path to global dominance in 1990, when it bought the Italian brand Vogue Eyewear.[133] A series of acquisitions of American firms followed, including Ray-Ban, Sunglass Hut and the discount retailers LensCrafters. Luxottica later increased its presence in the retail sector by acquiring Sydney-based OPSM in 2003, and Pearle Vision and its parent company, Cole National, in 2004. Finally, in 2017, Luxottica acquired its last major global competitor, Essilor, for €46 billion, in a merger that the European Commission inexplicably approved without conditions.[134]

Economists suggest you can see proof of monopoly power in the ability of a firm to sustain high prices far in excess of its costs – just as Luxottica has managed to. But if glasses and sunglasses don't actually cost that much to manufacture, what prevents a firm with a strong brand from dropping its prices and beating Luxottica? After all, classic economic theory suggests this should be possible.

It's true that Luxottica's prices are high enough to sustain a global market for ubiquitous knock-offs. It is also true that in Asia, Luxottica is much less of a player. Yet Luxottica manages to hold its market – luxury, branded glasses and sunglasses – by its combined strategy of owning the vast majority of the brands of relevance, controlling significant amounts of retail power, and severely punishing those who challenge it.

This was a lesson learned the hard way by the sports sunglasses manufacturer Oakley when it took a brief run at Luxottica by dropping its prices in the 2000s. Luxottica retaliated by dropping Oakley from its stores, which weakened the firm, then acquiring the company in a hostile takeover.[135] Perhaps unsurprisingly, given the climate, these manoeuvres received no serious scrutiny from competition officials. This is how global monopoly is maintained.

Eyewear is not the only industry to have undergone global consolidation. You might think of beer existing in a competitive market, but once again you'd be wrong. Over the past thirty years, the Belgian brewer Interbrew has grown from a local purveyor of beers into the world's dominant brewer. In an extraordinary campaign of global consolidation, the firm AB InBev has bought nearly every single major brewer in the world, as well as many of the leading craft breweries. As it stands, it owns most of the major breweries in the world; that is, those not owned by its main rival, Heineken, which owns most of the rest of the major beers of the world. Hence, nearly every major brand of beer you've heard of, such as Heineken, Stella Artois, Foster's, Budweiser, Amstel, Leffe and so on, is owned by two companies.

The global beer industry is, to be sure, being challenged by new craft brewers in the United States, parts of Europe and parts of South America. Many people prefer craft beers because the beer tastes better – a matter that industrial brewers were able to ignore for decades. But AB InBev and Heineken have not taken the rise of craft beers lying down. Instead, they've used lax laws to buy the largest craft breweries and try to make sure their own craft beers are the winners. Hence, in most countries around the world the most successful crafts are coming under the ownership of AB InBev and Heineken, dulling competition. Meanwhile, AB InBev has even begun buying the websites that rate and compare craft beers, further compromising the beer market.

One of the great problems with a global consolidation campaign like this is that national anti-monopoly

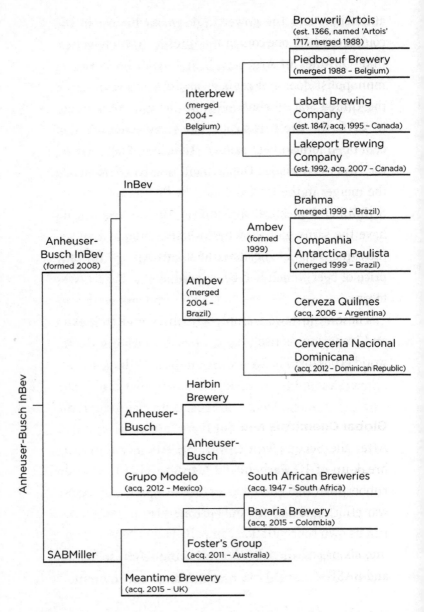

Figure 1: *Consolidations in the global beer industry – proof of the curse of bigness at work.*

authorities lack the power to respond effectively. In countries where one company is already the monopolist (like Quilmes in Argentina), its buyout by a global monopolist does not register as anticompetitive. In the United States, when AB InBev bought SABMiller in 2016, the two firms collectively controlled 75 per cent of American beer sales.[136] That figure compelled the American Justice Department to effectively block the merger in the United States (by forcing the sale of SABMiller domestically). However, the two firms still have the same global owner overseas, and still have the same corporate headquarters. Unsurprisingly, the price of beer, which had been going down, has begun to rise.

These are just two examples of global monopolization and important consolidations that have affected the world economy. The following are some of the others.

Global Chemicals and Seed

After the Second World War, the Allies forced the break-up of IG Farben, the German chemical and rubber firm that served as principal actor in Hitler's war effort, and also the only private firm in history to run its own concentration camp. IG Farben was broken into six pieces, the three largest being Bayer, Hoechst and BASF.[137]

Yet fast-forward to 2018, and Bayer has purchased Monsanto, the American chemical giant, to create the world's largest combined seed, fertilizer and chemical company.[138] It is part of a global chemical oligopoly, after the mergers of Dow and DuPont (both American firms),[139] and the acquisition of Syngenta by ChemChina.[140]

Airlines

In many countries, the promise of cheaper tickets, once promised by 'deregulation', has been countered by extensive consolidation of the industry. In the United States, for example, the industry has been reduced to just three major airlines: United, American and Delta, which maintain similar prices while putting more, smaller seats into planes, and raising fees.

Telecommunications

Around the world, nations have allowed their mobile telephone operators to consolidate into a small number of giant firms. For example, the European Commission approved the consolidation of carriers in Netherlands and Italy; the Indian market consolidated into four major firms; and in the United States, the federal government in 2019 signed off on a merger that would reduce the number of carriers to three.

The fiction of an international 'race to 5G' is often invoked to justify a reduction to just two or three carriers – the premise being that larger companies are needed to make the investments necessary to win the race. However, it is notable that two or three are also numbers which naturally make cooperation on prices much easier.

Pharmaceuticals

The pharmaceutical industry, which had been fairly fragmented, underwent a major consolidation from 1995 to 2015, with thousands of combinations that reduced the international market from some sixty-odd firms to about ten.[141] Meanwhile, within the United States, enforcement agencies allowed the passage of a new and disturbing kind of prescription drug acquisition: the sale of a drug to a firm whose immediate design was to take full advantage of the monopoly pricing potential. In some cases this meant raising prices by at least 1,000 per cent and sometimes as much as 6,000 per cent.[142] The most famous example was that of an opportunistic young man named Martin Shkreli who managed to acquire the facilities for the production of a drug named Daraprim, and immediately increased the price from $13.50 a pill to $750. That was just one of many similar transactions – none of which were challenged – and indeed the price of Daraprim remains at $750.

Why or how could any of this happen when so many nations have laws banning anticompetitive mergers? How could this happen under an American president, Barack Obama, who said he was committed to the antitrust laws,[143] and European Commissions who liked to style themselves as 'aggressive'?[144] Why have we allowed the dangerous economic structure of the 1930s to re-emerge, even in Europe, where Ordoliberal thought was once so influential?

The fact is that, around the world, the powerful influence of Chicago-School and neoliberal thinking has been accepted as the baseline, severely weakening the law's power. Robert Bork's idea that strict reliance on economic analysis was a mark of good character has become a controlling ideology. Price theory, and consumer welfare – the demand that government decisively prove the harmful effects of mergers in terms of effects on customer prices – has had its impact.

Yet of all the oversights of the past decade, the greatest was elsewhere. It lay in tech consolidation, which has allowed the almost entirely uninhibited consolidation of the 'new' Web industry into a new class of monopolists, possibly more powerful than any of their predecessors.

8

THE RISE OF
THE TECH GIANTS

Back in the 1990s and 2000s, when the Web and
the Internet were new, it felt like a golden age had
begun. The Internet and the Web formed a special
exception, not just to the laws of business but to just
about everything humanity had faced before. Personal
relationships, private identity and communication
styles were all different 'in cyberspace'. Logically, this
also suggested a change to the principles guiding
business and economics.

What else could one conclude when, in the 2000s,
a tiny blog could outdo an established media outlet?
When start-ups seemed to come from nowhere, gain
millions of users overnight, and make their founders
and employees wealthier than the old school tycoons?

The man who best described the mood was the author John Perry Barlow, who in the 1990s implored those interested in cyberspace to 'imagine a place where trespassers leave no footprints, where goods can be stolen an infinite number of times and yet remain in the possession of their original owners, where businesses you never heard of can own the history of your personal affairs, where only children feel completely at home, where the physics is that of thought rather than things, and where everyone is as virtual as the shadows in Plato's cave.'[145]

Everything was fast and chaotic; no position was lasting. One day, America's AOL was dominant and all-powerful; the next, it was the subject of business books mocking its many failures. Netscape rose and fell like a rocket that failed to achieve orbit (though Microsoft had something to do with that). Myspace, the social media pioneer, was everywhere, and then nowhere when Facebook came along.

The chaos made it easy to think that bigness – the economics of scale – no longer really mattered in the new economy. If anything, it seemed that being big, like being old, was just a disadvantage. Being big meant being hierarchical, industrial, dinosaur-like in an age of fleet-footed mammals. Better maybe to stay small and stay young, to 'move fast and break things', as the Silicon Valley mantra went.

All this suggested that in cyberspace, there could be no such thing as a lasting monopoly. The Internet would never stand for it. Business was now moving at Internet speed: a three-year-old firm was middle-aged; a five-year-old firm almost certainly near death. 'Barriers to entry' was a twentieth-century concept. Now, competition was always just 'one click away'.

It seemed that even if a firm did manage to gain temporary dominance, there was nothing to be afraid of. We were not speaking of the evil monopolists of old. The new firms were instead devoted to spreading sweetness and light, goodwill to all men – whether access to information (Google), good books for cheap (Amazon) or the building of a global community (Facebook). Not only did they not charge high prices, sometimes they didn't even charge at all. Google would give you free email, free map apps, free cloud storage. Hence, businesses like Facebook or Google were seen as more akin to a charity. And who would sue the Red Cross?

In these heady times, only a malcontent would dare suggest that just maybe, business and economics had not quite been reinvented forever. Or that what was taken to be a new order might, in fact, just be a phase that was destined to come to an end as firms better understood the market and its new technologies. The good times were on, or so it seemed.

But after a decade of open chaos and easy market entry, something surprising did happen. As the 2010s began, a few firms – Google, Facebook and Amazon – did not disappear. They hit that five-year mark of obsolescence with no signs of impending collapse or retirement. Instead, the major firms seemed to be sticking, and even growing in their dominance. Suddenly, there weren't a dozen search engines, each with a different idea, but a single search engine. There were no longer hundreds of stores that everyone went to, but one 'everything store'. And to avoid Facebook was to make yourself a digital hermit. There stopped being a next new thing, or at least, a new thing that was a serious challenge to the old thing.

Unfortunately, the officials who are supposed to control competition failed to notice that the 1990s were over. Instead, for a decade and counting, it gave the major tech players a pass – even when confronting fairly obvious red flags and anticompetitive mergers. That is best exemplified by the Facebook story.

Launched in 2004, Facebook quickly dispatched its main American rival, Myspace, which had been a rare Los Angeles tech success story, but had become a mess of intrusive advertising, fake users and trolls. In just a few years, Facebook achieved an early dominance over general purpose social networking.

By the 2010s, Facebook faced one of its most serious challengers, a start-up named Instagram. Instagram combined a photo and video app with a social network on which it was easy and fast to share content on mobile phones. It was popular with younger people, and it was not long before some of its advantages over Facebook were noticed. As business writer Nicholas Carlson said at the time, Instagram 'allows people to do what they like to do on Facebook easier and faster'.[146]

Having already gained thirty million users in just eighteen months of existence, Instagram was poised to become a leading challenger to Facebook due to its strength on mobile platforms, where Facebook was weak. By the doctrine of Internet time, Facebook, then eight years old, was supposed to be heading into retirement.

This disruption narrative was rudely interrupted. Instead of surrendering to the inevitable, Facebook realized it could just buy out the new. For just $1 billion, Facebook eliminated its existential problem and reassured its investors. As *Time* would put it, 'Buying Instagram conveyed to investors that the company was serious about dominating the mobile ecosystem while also neutralizing a nascent competitor.'[147]

When a dominant firm buys its challenger, alarm bells are supposed to ring. Yet both American and European regulators found themselves unable to find anything wrong with the takeover. The American analysis remains secret, but we have the United Kingdom's report. Its analysis, such as it was, went as follows: Facebook did not have a photo-taking app, meaning that Facebook was not competing with Instagram for consumers. Instagram did not have advertising revenue, so it did not compete with Facebook either. Hence, the report was able to reach the extraordinary conclusion that Facebook and Instagram were not competitors.[148]

It takes many years of training to reach conclusions this absurd. A teenager could have told you that Facebook and Instagram were competitors – after all, teenagers were the ones who were switching platforms. With this level of insight, the world's governments in the 2010s did nothing to stop the largest firms from buying everyone and anyone who might be a potential threat.

Nothing was learned from the Instagram failure. Using an app which allowed it to spy on the usage habits of millions of users, Facebook began to believe that WhatsApp was a serious threat to its business. WhatsApp had a stronger global presence, and it promised a more secure messaging-centred service. So Facebook offered a suspiciously enormous $19 billion buyout – which somehow failed to raise any real alarm.[149] At the time, many were shocked at the price.

But when one is actually agreeing to split a monopoly as ludicrous as generalized social media, with over $50 billion in annual revenue, the price suddenly makes sense.[150]

In total, Facebook managed to string together more than 90 unchallenged acquisitions, which seems impressive, until you consider that Google got away with at least 270.[151] In this way, the tech industry became largely composed of just a few giant trusts: Google for search and related industries, Facebook for social media, and, in the United States, Amazon for online commerce. While competitors remained in the wings, their positions became marginalized with every passing day.

While many of these acquisitions were small, or mere 'acqui-hires' (i.e. acquisitions to hire employees), others, like Facebook's takeover of Instagram and WhatsApp, eliminated serious competitive threats. In the 2000s, Google had launched Google Video and done pretty well, but not compared to its greatest competitor, YouTube. Google bought YouTube without a peep from the competition agencies. Waze, an upstart online mapping company, was poised to be a catalyst for Google's challengers, until Google, the owner of its own dominant online mapping program, bought the firm in a fairly blatant merger to monopoly. Google also acquired AdMob, its most serious competitor for online advertising, which the US government let happen on the basis that Apple might also enter the market in a serious way (it didn't). Meanwhile, Amazon acquired would-be competitors like Zappos, Diapers.com and Soap.com.

These were hardly coercive takeovers. Most of these firms were happy to have a big fat buyout. But if the takeovers were friendlier, their net effect was the continued domination by the trusts. This was obvious to the business press. As TechCrunch opined of the 2014 WhatsApp acquisition, 'Facebook [now] possesses the most popular messaging app, and has neutralized the biggest threat to its global domination of social networking.'[152] Or as another business analyst wrote at the time: 'Without this acquisition, "uncool" Facebook would have been in a very difficult competitive position against its cooler messaging apps rivals [which] would have posed an existential threat for Facebook. By acquiring the leader in messaging apps, Facebook has removed this threat.'[153]

Where buyouts were not practical, the tech firms tried a different approach: cloning, the favourite tactic of Microsoft back in the day. Faced with a potential competitive challenge from Yelp's popular reviews of local businesses in the early 2010s, Google created its own local sites attached to Google maps. The value in any such site would rest in the quality of its user reviews, and as a newcomer, Google didn't have any of those. It solved the problem by simply purloining Yelp's reviews and putting them on its site, making Yelp essentially redundant, and also harvesting the proceeds of its many years of work.[154]

Meanwhile, Facebook cloned so many of its rival Snapchat's features that it began to seem like a running joke – most importantly, its 'stories' feature. Amazon has a track record of cloning products that succeed so it can help itself to the margins. To be sure, there is nothing wrong with firms copying to learn from each other; that's how innovation can happen. But there is a line where copying and exclusion becomes anticompetitive, where the goal becomes the maintenance of monopoly as opposed to real improvement. When Facebook spies on competitors or summons a firm to a meeting just to figure out how to copy it more accurately, or discourages funding of competitors, a line is crossed.

Over the years, as with the original trust movement, a strong current of self-justification began to creep into the consolidation. This made things somewhat awkward for some of the firms who, as start-ups, had been committed to the old Internet ideals of openness and chaos. Now it was all for the best; a law of nature, a chance for the monopolists to do good for the universe. The cheerer-in-chief for the monopoly form was PayPal founder and billionaire Peter Thiel, author of a tract entitled 'Competition is for Losers'. Labelling the competitive economy a 'relic of history' and a 'trap', he proclaimed that 'only one thing can allow a business to transcend the daily brute struggle for survival: monopoly profits.'[155]

The big tech firms are a little more circumspect than Thiel. For Facebook, it is not trying to build a global empire of influence so much as 'bringing the world closer together'. It is supposedly a 'different kind of company that connects billions of people'.[156] To do that right, however, requires a global monopoly. Meanwhile, Google wants to organize the world's information, but to do so it needs to get its hands on all the information in the world. Amazon, meanwhile, wants nothing more than to serve the consumer, which is great, and you can check out any time you like, but you can never leave. If there is a sector more ripe for the reinvigoration of the big case tradition, I do not know it.

China's Tech Champions

If the United States has allowed monopolies to emerge across the tech industry and to buy out their challengers, China has taken a different approach: the active cultivation and promotion of its own, home-grown tech monopolies. By one count, nine of the world's twenty largest tech firms are Chinese.[157]

Along the way, the Chinese government has also found occasion to mix private and public power in a manner that can only be described as alarming.

Central planning, of course, is nothing new to the Chinese state. From the 1950s through the 1980s, China subscribed to an economic model based on the Soviet Union's and reflected the influence both of Stalinist and Leninist thinking. By the 1960s, most of China's major companies were state-owned, usually monopolies, and a Stalinist process of central planning centred on five-year plans determined what would be produced by whom.

That, at the risk of understatement, did not go well. Beginning in 1979, after a few disastrous decades (and several million deaths via starvation), China left much of the old model behind – but did keep parts of it. Stalin's coercive economic planning is gone, as is the ban on private property and private investment. But Lenin's concept of the Communist Party as the director of the economy remains intact. Hence, the economy is capitalist, but still directed, at some level, by the party-state. This has made China into something like a much more successful version of Mussolini's economic model, where a strong state oversees a powerful private sector.

China's tech sector is, in particular, a by-product of state involvement and encouragement. To be sure, China has a highly talented class of software engineers and scientists, an entrepreneurial culture, and a citizenry that has rapidly embraced new technologies, sometimes leapfrogging earlier generations of technology. And it is also true that its tech sector has more competition than other parts of the Chinese economy. But China might only be a middling tech power if not for several types of state intervention. For one thing, most of the major American tech platforms are either blocked (Facebook, Twitter) or heavily disadvantaged (Google). That, along with extensive state subsidization – tech is regularly included in China's 'five-year plans' – has fertilized the growth of domestic giants. These include China Mobile, the state-owned mobile operator; Tencent, the giant of social media, an equivalent to Facebook and Twitter; Alibaba, which is like a combination of eBay, Amazon and PayPal; Baidu, China's leading search engine (Google left the country in the 2010s concerned that it was being spied on and having its technologies stolen); and Huawei, which makes phones and Internet equipment.

A nation's incubation of its own competitors is not necessarily a bad thing; in fact, it is surprising that more countries haven't successfully done the same thing in their Internet sector. But there is a line between incubation and insulation. What makes the Chinese story distinct is the degree to which the state has come to use its monopolists for its own purposes, and the entwining of the party-state and its major tech giants.

Consider, for example, WeChat, China's leading messaging and social networking mobile app, with over one billion users. One journalist described WeChat as 'the equivalent of WhatsApp plus Facebook plus PayPal plus Uber plus Grubhub plus many other things'.[158] It has become essential in China, the one app that no one can live without, unless wishing to live as a hermit. Many people describe themselves as 'living' on WeChat.

While it is a private company, WeChat – and Tencent, the parent company – have become increasingly close to the Chinese state. Tencent, for example, was named as one of China's official 'AI champions' in 2018, and it regularly receives various forms of subsidies, large and small.[159] But the favours go both ways: in recent years, the state has announced plans to integrate a national ID system into WeChat. Also, though the accusations are denied, China is widely understood to use WeChat as a surveillance tool, to spy on anyone from criminals to potential dissidents; there are records of the Chinese state arresting people based on WeChat messages.[160] In an Amnesty International survey of the privacy practices of the world's major tech platforms, Tencent scored 0 out of 100, the lowest of any firm.[161] This is the very mixed picture of the Chinese tech economy.

As of this writing, China is one of the very few countries to have its own fully developed domestic tech sector. But as the state increases its active control and direction of these firms, the question is whether China may end up in the same situation as Japan in the 1980s and 1990s. Will this generation of tech companies become too entrenched, too much like state industry? China, in some ways, is hoping that its party leadership can guess the future of tech, which is why, for example, it has bet so heavily on 'next generation AI' and similar technologies.

It may, to many, seem like a great idea, now at least. But it is worth remembering that Japan, in the 1980s, was sure that supercomputers were the future. But history shows that big bets are just that, and they create dangers for any economy that comes to rely heavily on just a few companies – as opposed to an ecosystem of competition, which, despite its chaos, remains the most stable form of economy the world has seen to date.

How America and the Rest of the World Respond

It may not be surprising to learn that the leaders of the American tech industry have not embraced the break-ups of their own companies. The argument they've presented merits special attention, for it invokes fears of Chinese domination and calls for an American return to the promotion of national champions, and a break with the tradition that had previously called for break-ups of tech monopolies.

Mark Zuckerberg of Facebook and other tech leaders offered a stark warning to those who might want more competition in the tech industries. It goes like this: 'We understand that we've made mistakes. But don't you realize that if we damage the current tech giants, we'll just be handing over the future to China? Unlike us, the Chinese government is standing behind its tech firms, because it knows that competition is global, and it wants to win.'[162] Some add that at least firms like Facebook and Google were founded in a place (California) with progressive ideals and democratic values. A future dominated by China would be far worse for the individual rights that we value.

This is Big Tech's version of the 'too big to fail' argument. Its appeal is superficial and nationalistic. It may also appeal to some who believe in an 'us versus them' narrative, who argue that a showdown between East and West is inevitable.

The Chinese tech sector is growing. It is aggressively competitive, and many of its firms enjoy the embrace and promotion of the Chinese state. That would seem to suggest a global contest for global dominance, one in which the United States ought not to be considering break-ups or regulation, but rather doing everything it can to protect and subsidize the 'good guys'.

But to accept this viewpoint would be wrong-headed. For one thing, there is no principle of nature that makes Western or American monopolists better or less dangerous than their Chinese counterparts. In the history of the last two hundred years, there are many villains. It would also betray and ignore hard-won lessons, discussed in this book, on the folly of an industrial policy centred on 'national champions', especially in the tech sector. What Facebook is really asking for is to be embraced and protected as the West's very own social media monopolist, as it does battle overseas. But both history and basic economics suggest we do much better trusting that fierce competition actually makes companies better, both technologically and in terms of what they have to offer customers.

There are real risks implicit in a governmental embrace of firms like Facebook, Apple and Google that should not be ignored. Take Facebook and Google together. These two firms hold more private information about the world's population than any other entities on earth. They also, collectively, have an apparent power to influence elections; perhaps not to decide them, but enough to swing a close vote. Should that power come into the hands of an entity determined to stay in office forever, the consequences could be truly alarming. It may begin, innocuously enough, with the idea that tech is doing its national duty as it aids the state. But it is apparent, based on the history of monopoly in the last century, that this is indeed the road to serfdom.

The story of the tech industries should not just be a story of the United States and China. Yet with the exception of a handful of other countries, including Israel, Japan, Taiwan and the Scandinavian nations, very few countries have successfully developed domestic tech industries of real significance. It is unusual for the world to be ruled not just by domestic monopolies, but fully global monopolies. The question for the rest of the world is, does all comparative advantage lie with only two countries? Over the next decade, if wealth is to be more evenly distributed, more of the world must find ways to make it in an industry that threatens to 'eat everything'.

CONCLUSION: BREAKING UP GLOBAL ECONOMIC POWER

This book has made its warning clear. If we do not do something about the ongoing concentration of global economic power, we face the real dangers of repeating the most dangerous mistakes of the twentieth century. There are many reasons to think that the supremacy of global monopolies will yield to further unrest, further support for radical, nationalistic leaders, and possibly much worse.

What should be done? There is no simple answer, but what is missing is an agenda dedicated to both braking and breaking private power, not just tinkering at the edges. It is not enough to demand change without providing an agenda that enjoys legal legitimacy, can make use of the best economic tools, and is usable by enforcers, judges and industry itself. That is the aspiration of this last chapter.

1. Mergers

The single greatest priority for a global anti-monopoly programme is the reform of how nations and the world approach mergers. In theory, many of the industrialized nations of the world have tough restrictions meant to prevent the emergence of monopolies and tight oligopolies. The American Anti-Merger Act of 1950, for example, was meant to erect a barrier to a 'rising tide of economic concentration' and therefore provided 'authority for arresting mergers at a time when the trend to a lessening of competition in a line of commerce was still in its incipiency'.[163] Europe's merger review authority is supposed to prevent mergers that create 'a concentration that would significantly impede effective competition' based on 'the creation or strengthening [of] a dominant position'.[164]

Yet merger control has wandered so far from these expressed intents as to make a mockery of the laws. Under the influence of a long obsession with pricing, the authorities have read into this language something that is obviously not in the text of the law: a general requirement that clear proof of higher prices after the merger be provided.

Ye shall know them by their fruits – and the bottom line is that, for two decades, the merger laws of the major nations have utterly failed to block a generation of anticompetitive mergers. The United States and Europe are equally guilty of accepting mergers that have undeniably diminished competition and squeezed workers and suppliers without much benefit.

Many of the worst examples are found in the United States. For example, across America, hospitals have merged, creating higher prices (in what is already the world's most expensive healthcare system) and also poorer performance, measured by patient mortality rates. In other words, patients pay more, but die more often.

Yet the Europeans cannot be let off the hook, for Europe has a bad habit of being too easily mollified. The Commission rarely blocks mergers outright, and thereby allows mergers that produce obvious monopolies or tight oligopolies. We've already described the 2016 decision by which Europe blessed a merger between the world's two largest beer companies, Anheuser-Busch InBev and SABMiller, to create a global beer monopolist headquartered in Belgium, which controls some five hundred brands of beer in a hundred countries. It was a merger so outrageous that even the American Justice Department effectively blocked it, at least within the United States.[165]

In Europe, authorities have far too often become comfortable with the idea that mergers will presumptively be approved, provided that concessions are made. Admittedly, it is true that in 2019 the Commission blocked a few notable mergers, such as the effort by the railway branch of Germany's Siemens and France's Alstom to create a single train-manufacturing monopolist.[166] But more generally in Europe there have been far too many mergers of the kind that even the United States would block.

High tech is its own problem, and Europe and the United States have both repeatedly failed to prevent anticompetitive mergers. The fact that a merger may be designed to eliminate a future or nascent competitor is often ignored as too speculative. That's why American and European agencies allowed Facebook and Google to buy many of their major potential competitors. Innovation and dynamic effects, being harder to measure, do not get due consideration.

One solution is obvious: passing much tougher standards for mergers, especially the mega-mergers – those of over $10 billion in size – that reshape industries. Given the stakes, there is no reason that the mega-merger should have the same standards. Instead, those proposing the union should face the burden of proving that the deal will not raise prices, stifle innovation or inflict other harms on the public.

Questionable mergers should be put 'on parole' – that is, reinvestigated after five years, and dissolved if obviously anticompetitive.

But none of these domestic measures is enough to deal with the problem of global monopolization. For through a series of cross-border acquisitions can be built a power which is truly beyond the purview or control of any individual nation. Like the international cartels before the Second World War, the global monopoly inhabits something akin to its own sovereignty and can have a power that rivals or exceeds smaller governments. Fighting global monopoly will therefore require new forms of cooperation between nations on behalf of their publics.

2. Market Investigations and Deconcentration

In 2007, the UK, using a device known as the 'market investigation', studied the conditions of competition among airports in London and Edinburgh, and concluded that the joint ownership of Heathrow, Gatwick, Stansted and four other airports was neither necessary nor serving the public. It proposed a divestiture that left the major airports competing for business: especially Heathrow, Gatwick and Stansted.[167] While strenuously resisted and fought in the British courts, the results have been widely lauded, yielding higher service quality and greater efficiency by various measures.

More countries should adopt a market investigations law like that of the UK. The prerequisite would be persistent dominance of at least ten years or longer, suggesting that a market remedy is not forthcoming, and proof that the existing industry structure lacked convincing competitive or public justifications, and that market forces would be unlikely to remedy the situation by themselves. In practice, the agency would put an overly consolidated industry under investigation, recommend remedies through the administration process, and adopt them, subject to judicial review. The market investigation would serve as a particularly effective tool for stagnant and long-standing but not particularly abusive or aggressive monopolies or duopolies.

3. Big Cases and Break-Ups

The American tradition of 'trustbusting' called for periodic investigation and break-ups of long-standing monopolies. But that tradition has been lost. It is time to bring back the big cases seeking the big, industry-resetting break-up. The great advantage of break-ups, done right, is that they have clear effects. They can completely realign an industry's incentives, and can, at their best, transform a stagnant industry into a dynamic one.

Most of the world has been far too reluctant to seek break-ups. The Europeans and Japanese, and even now the Americans, too often portray break-ups and dissolutions as off the table or only for extremely rare cases. They tend to prefer highly intellectualized remedies that are meant to restore competition, yet in practice rarely do.

European officials have an enviable tendency to start important cases, particularly in the tech area, where they have become the principal overseers of the American tech industries. Europe deserves credit for the fact that it now leads in the scrutiny of 'big tech', including the case against Google's practices, and in smaller, less public matters, like policing how Apple deals with competitors who also depend on the iPhone platform.

Unfortunately, Europe does not conclude these cases well. As an example, Europe chased Microsoft around for years, but instead of aiming for a break-up (as the Americans had), they pursued a remedy centred on the dominance of the Windows Media Player and forced Microsoft to give its users the option of choosing different media players upon installation. Nobody did so – it was a classic example of a failed remedy.[168]

In the United States, too much of the resistance to dissolution comes from taking too seriously the legal fiction of corporate personhood. In reality, a large corporation is made up of sub-units, whether functional or regional, or independent operations that have been previously acquired. It is not impossible to administer a break-up as is sometimes claimed. Many break-ups are akin to the spin-offs or dissolutions that are not uncommon in business practice as it stands.

The same logic also suggests more retrospective consideration of consummated mergers – that is, dissolutions initiated some years after a merger is completed. Over the last few decades the American agencies have, to some degree, increased their volume of investigation into consummated mergers, and this is a welcome development. The basic premise is that the actual effects of a merger can be assessed more accurately than any prediction. To target a consummated merger that has become a major detriment to the public is very much in the anti-monopoly spirit of the laws.

Consider a break-up of Facebook that reassessed the mergers with Instagram and WhatsApp. While doubtlessly Facebook would oppose such a dissolution, and find the new competition unwelcome, it is hard to see what the great social cost, if any, would be. It is not clear that there are important social efficiencies gained by the combination of these firms. But reintroducing competition into the social media space, perhaps even quality competition, measured by matters like greater protection of privacy, could mean a lot to the public. We have not even touched upon the non-economic concerns, such as the concentration of so much power over speech into a single platform.

Efforts to break up companies will always encounter resistance, not least from the target itself. What no one can question is that break-ups have real consequences. Done right, they can shake up a stagnant industry, inspire new competitors to enter, and reshuffle the deck. At their best, they can even change the very nature of a country's political economy, by splintering industries with too much control over politics into more discrete, less powerful pieces. Nor are break-ups somehow a death sentence to the national economy. The economies of Germany and Japan were transformed by perhaps the most ambitious series of corporate break-ups in world history. Yet both remain better versions of themselves, and among the wealthiest nations in the world.

4. The Goals

There is good reason to think that anti-monopoly's intended economic and political roles cannot be fully recovered without its narrow focus on prices and microeconomics – as if this is all that matters to people. If this book has shown something, it should be that the stakes are very large when it comes to private power, that economics and politics are closely linked, and that the cultivation of monopoly can be dangerous for democracy.

Nonetheless, much of the world has accepted the Chicago School's idea that 'consumer welfare' is the lodestone of the law, and nothing else matters. It is time to leave that behind – accept that the standard has failed, and adopt a framework more reflective of the law's traditional range of concerns.

What would a believer in Ordoliberalism or Brandeisian law do? Personally, I advocate what is called the 'protection of competition' test. It is one that adopts the 'gardener' model of the state in the economy, trying to protect a healthy process of competition and market functioning. It asks the state to eliminate subversions and abuses of a healthy market system. This kind of analysis attempts to capture far more of the dynamics of the competitive process than do existing analyses, and also implicates political considerations as well. It is well captured in what Brandeis once wrote of all restraints of competition: '[t]he true test of legality is whether the restraint imposed is such as merely regulates, and perhaps thereby promotes competition, or whether it is such as may suppress or even destroy competition. . .'[169]

5. Redistribution of Monopoly Profit

Many of the nations in the world have chosen to accept monopolization or tight oligopoly in major industries. I would think this an unwise course over the longer term, and that a broader ecosystem is preferable. If nations are to accept this arrangement – accept monopoly profit – a basic logic suggests they should also accept a much greater duty of redistribution to the broader populace.

As it stands, matters have actually moved in the opposite direction. Most European nations do not tax corporate profit, and the United States has cut its corporate tax rates. The wealthiest corporation in the entire world, Amazon, pays nothing in taxes on its profit, and in fact gets money from the American federal government.[170]

A policy that gives more to those who already have more seems destined to lead in dangerous directions, for reasons we have already discussed at length in this book. Hence, the need for a deep rethinking of redistribution in an era that tolerates so much concentrated private power, and so much profit.

This book does not present an agenda for solving every economic challenge produced by the new Gilded Age in which we live. But it demands that something be done. It recognizes that structure matters, and pleads for an economic vision that prizes dynamism and possibility, and that, ultimately, attunes economic structure to a democratic society.

The English Magna Carta, the Constitution of the United States, the Treaty of Lisbon and the United Nations Charter were all created with the idea that power should be limited – that it should be distributed, decentralized, checked and balanced, so that no person or institution could enjoy unaccountable influence.

Yet these visions share a major flaw. Written as a reaction to government tyranny, they do not contemplate the possibility of concentrated private power that might come to rival the public's, of business people with more influence than government officials, and of an artificial creature of law – the corporation – that would grow to have political protection exceeding that of actual humans. Nor did they contemplate global, consolidated corporations with more power than nation states.

The struggle for democracy needs to turn to the control of private power – both by itself, and also in its influence over, and union with, government power. Louis Brandeis viewed a true democracy as one composed of liberties and securities, so as to enable human flourishing in a nation of rough economic equals. It is a challenging balance to get right. But if we know one thing, it is that we have drifted very far from a defensible division of the spoils of progress or the kind of economic security that yields human flourishing.

ACKNOWLEDGEMENTS

I wish to acknowledge the work of my editor James Pulford, my agents Tina Bennett, Fiona Baird and Svetlana Katz, my copyeditor David Inglesfield, and my research assistants Hillary L. Hubley, Peter Cramer and Taylor Sutton. I thank my beloved wife Kate and offer a special thanks to my two daughters Sierra and Essie, without whose assistance and encouragement this book would have been finished much earlier.

NOTES

1 A. B. Atkinson, 'The Distribution of Top Incomes in the United Kingdom 1908–2000', in A. B. Atkinson and T. Piketty (eds.), *Top Incomes Over the Twentieth Century*, New York, Oxford University Press, 2007, p. 95.

2 Facundo Alvaredo, Anthony B. Atkinson, Thomas Piketty and Emmanuel Saez, 'The Top 1 Percent in International and Historical Perspective', *Journal of Economic Perspectives*, vol. 27, no. 3, Summer 2013, p. 3.

3 Ibid., p. 7; A. B. Atkinson and J. E. Søgaard, 'The Long Run History of Income Inequality in Denmark', ERPU Working Paper Series (2013), p. 24; Bas van Bavel and Ewout Frankema, 'Wealth Inequality in the Netherlands, *c.* 1950–2015: The Paradox of a Northern European Welfare State', *Low Countries Journal of Social and Economic History*, vol. 14, no. 2, 2017, p. 53.

4 James Davis, Rodrigo Lluberas and Anthony Shorrocks, 'Credit Suisse Global Wealth Databook 2018', *Credit Suisse Global Wealth Report 2018*, October 2018, p. 9.

5 Nomi Prins, 'The Rich Are Still Getting Richer', *The Nation*, 26 February 2019.

6 'Global Income Inequality Dynamics', Part II: Trends in Global Income Inequality, World Inequality Lab, https://wir2018.wid.world/ part-2.html, (accessed 14 November 2019).

7 United Nations Conference on Trade and Development (UNCTAD), 'Beyond Austerity: Towards a Global New Deal', *Trade and Development Report 2017*, 2017, p. 15.

8 Gustavo Grullon, Yelena Larkin and Roni Michaely, 'Are US Industries Becoming More Concentrated?', *Review of Finance*, vol. 23, no. 4, April 2017, p. 697.

9 Juan Forero, 'Brazilian Company JBS Dominates Beef Industry from Farm to Fork', *Washington Post*, 14 April 2011.

10 Ibid.

11 Forero, 'JBS Dominates Beef Industry'.

12 Philip H. Howard, 'Corporate Concentration in Global Meat Processing: The Role of Government Subsidies', Michigan State University (September 2017), p. 1; Luke Runyon, 'Inside the World's Largest Food Company You've Probably Never Heard of', *Civil Eats*, 30 June 2015.

13 Karla Mendes, 'Brazil's "Chicken Catchers" Are Victims of Forced Labor: Report', Reuters, 30 November 2017.

14 Rogerio Jelmayer and Luciana Magalhaes, 'Brazil Police Search Home of JBS Chief, Parent Company's Headquarters', *Wall Street Journal*, 1 July 2016.

15 David Meyer, 'JBS Batista Brothers Arrested as Brazil Corruption Probes Spiral', *Fortune*, 14 September 2017; Luciana Magalhaes and Paul Kiernan, 'JBS Parent to Pay $3.2 Billion to Settle Corruption Investigations in Brazil', *Wall Street Journal*, 31 May 2017.

16 Joe Leahy, 'BNDES: Lender of First Resort for Brazil's Tycoons', *Financial Times*, 11 January 2015.

17 'Brazil's Recession Worst on Record', BBC, 7 March 2017.

18 Dom Phillips, 'Outrage after Brazil Ministry Asks Schools to Read Aloud Bolsonaro Slogan', *Guardian*, 26 February 2019.

19 Walter K. Bennett, 'Some Reflections on the Interpretation of the Sherman Act Since the Emergency', *Federal Bar Journal*, vol. 8, no. 4, July 1947, p. 317.

20 U.S. Congress, Senate, Committee on Military Affairs, Subcommittee on War Mobilization, *Cartels and National Security: Report Pursuant to S. Res. 107*, 78th Cong., 2d sess., 1944, Subcomm. Rep 4, 8.

21 Military Governor for Germany (U.S.), Proclamation, 'Prohibition of Excessive Concentration of German Economic Power; Law No. 56', *Federal Register*, vol. 12, no. 212, 29 October 1947, p. 7001.

NOTES

22 Hermann Levy, *Industrial Germany: A Study of Its Monopoly Organisations and Their Control by the State*, Cambridge, Cambridge University Press, 2013, p. 7.

23 'Kilgore Asks Labor Own Reich Industry', *New York Times*, 2 October 1944.

24 Knut Wolfgang Nörr, 'Franz Böhm and the Theory of the Private Law Society', in Peter Koslowski (ed.), *The Theory of Capitalism in the German Economic Tradition: Historism, Ordo-Liberalism, Critical Theory, Solidarism*, New York, Springer, 2000, p. 150.

25 Herbert Spencer, *Social Statics: or, the Conditions Essential to Happiness Specified, and the First of Them Developed*, London, John Chapman, 1851, p. 379.

26 Ibid., p. 416.

27 Gustav Schmoller, 'Das Verhältnis der Kartelle zum Staate', *Jahrbuch für Gesetzgebung, Verwaltung und Volkswirtschaft im Deutschen Reich*, vol. 29 (1905), p. 359, quoted and translated in Holm Arno Leonhardt, *The Development of Cartel+ Theory Between 1883 and the 1930s*, Hildesheim, Universitätsverlag Hildesheim, 2018, p. 38.

28 Knut Wolfgang Nörr, 'Law and Market Organization: The Historical Experience in Germany From 1900 to the Law Against Restraints of Competition (1957)', *Journal of Institutional and Theoretical Economics*, vol. 151, no. 1, March 1995, p. 8.

29 Ibid., pp. 5–20.

30 Adolf Hitler to Hermann Göring, memorandum, August 1936, cited in R. J. Overy, *The Dictators: Hitler's Germany and Stalin's Russia*, New York, W. W. Norton & Co., 2004, p. 441.

31 Hitler, memorandum, cited in R. J. Overy, 'Misjudging Hitler', in Gordon Martel (ed.), *The Origins of the Second World War Reconsidered*, London, Routledge, 1999, p. 103.

32 Franz Böhm, 'Decartelisation and De-concentration: A Problem for Specialists or a Fateful Question?', in Thomas Biebricher and Frieder Vogelmann (eds.), *The Birth of Austerity: German Ordoliberalism and Contemporary Neoliberalism*, New York, Rowman & Littlefield International, 2017, p. 133.

33 U.S. Congress, Senate, Committee on Military Affairs, *Elimination of German Resources for War: Hearings Before a Subcommittee of the Committee for Military Affairs*, 78th and 79th Cong., p. 1067.

34 Young Namkoong, 'Impact of the Zaibatsu on Japan's Political Economy: Pre and Post War Period', *International Area Review*, vol. 9, no. 2, June 2006.

35 Ibid.

36 Iwasaki Koyota, quoted in Johannes Hirschmeier and Tusenehiko Yui, *The Development of Japanese Business: 1600–1973*, New York, Routledge, 1975, p. 223.

37 Corwin Edwards, 'The Dissolution of the Japanese Combines', *Pacific Affairs*, vol. 19, no. 3, September 1946, pp. 228–9.

38 Corwin Edwards, 'Report of the Mission on Japanese Combines: Part I Analytical and Technical Data', quoted in Yoneyuki Sugita, *Pitfall or Panacea: The Irony of US Power in Occupied Japan, 1945–1952*, New York, Routledge, 2003, p. 24.

39 Cartels and National Security: Report from the Subcommittee on War Mobilization to the Committee on Military Affairs, United States Senate, Pursuant to S. Res. 107, 78th Cong., 1944, Part I.

40 'The Threat to Democracy', *New Republic*, vol. 110, no. 7, 14 February 1944, pp. 199–200.

41 *Thompson v. Haight*, 23 F. Cas. 1040, pp. 1042–43 (C.C.S.D.N.Y. 1826).

42 The Case of Monopolies (1602) 77 Eng. Rep. 1260, 1262 (QB).

43 Statute of Monopolies, 1623, 21 Jac. 1, c. 3.

44 Levy, *Industrial Germany*, pp. 5, 7.

45 Ibid., p. 7.

46 Richard Frothingham, *Life and Times of Joseph Warren*, Boston, Little, Brown and Co., 1865, p. 255.

47 Dana Frank, *Buy American: The Untold Story of Economic Nationalism*, Boston, Beacon Press, 2000, p. 3.

48 George Hewes, 'An Account of the Boston Tea Party (1773)', in Randall M. Miller (ed.), *Daily Life Through American History in Primary Documents*, Santa Barbara, ABC-CLIO, 2012, Vol. 1, p. 210.

49 Robert J. Allison, foreword to *The Boston Tea Party*, Carlisle, Commonwealth Editions, 2007, p. v; Thomas Hutchinson, *The Diary and Letters of His Excellency Thomas Hutchinson*, Carlisle, Applewood Books, 2010, Vol. 1, p. 139.

50 Steven G. Calabresi and Larissa Price, 'Monopolies and the Constitution: A History of Crony Capitalism', *Northwestern University School of Law Scholarly Commons*, 2012.

51 Neil H. Cogan, *The Complete Bill of Rights: The Drafts, Debates, Sources, and Origins*, New York, Oxford University Press, 2015, p. 179.

52 Jeffrey Rosen, *Louis D. Brandeis: American Prophet*, New Haven, Yale University Press, 2016, pp. 30–31.

53 Melvin I. Urofsky, *Louis D. Brandeis: A Life*, New York, Pantheon, 2009.

54 Ibid.

55 Michael C. Jensen, 'The Modern Industrial Revolution, Exit, and the Failure of Internal Control Systems', *Journal of Applied Corporate Finance*, vol. 22, no. 1 (2010); C. Paul Rogers III, 'A Concise History of Corporate Mergers and Antitrust Laws in the United States', *National Law School of India Review*, vol. 24, no. 2, 2013.

56 Thomas A. Barnico, 'Brandeis, Choate and the Boston & Maine Merger Battle, 1903–1914', *Massachusetts Legal History* 3, 1997.

57 Urofsky, *Louis D. Brandeis: A Life*, pp. 8–9.

58 Ibid., p. 182.

59 Louis D. Brandeis, 'New England Railroad Situation', *Boston Journal*, 13 December 1912.

60 *Control of Corporations, Persons, and Firms Engaged in Interstate Commerce: Hearings Pursuant to S. Res. 98, Before the Committee on Interstate Commerce*, 62d Cong. 1174 (1912) (statement of Louis D. Brandeis, Esq., Attorney at Law, of Boston, Mass.).

61 Louis D. Brandeis, 'True Americanism' (speech, Boston, MA, 5 July 1915), Louis D. Brandeis School of Law Library, https://louisville.edu/law/library/special-collections/the-louis-d.-brandeis-collection/business-a-profession-chapter-22, (accessed 20 December 2019).

62 Robert Devigne, *Reforming Liberalism: J. S. Mill's Use of Ancient, Religious, Liberal, and Romantic Moralities*, New Haven, Yale University Press, 2006, p. 76.

63 Louis D. Brandeis, 'True Americanism'.

64 Louis D. Brandeis, 'Efficiency and Social Ideals', *Independent* (New York, NY), 30 November 1914.

65 *Whitney v. California*, 274 U.S. 357, 375 (Brandeis, J. concurring), 1927.

66 Louis D. Brandeis, 'True Americanism'.

67 Louis D. Brandeis, 'The New Slavery' (speech, New York, NY, 3 February 1912), quoted in *American Marine Engineer*, April 1912.

68 Thomas K. McCraw, 'Louis D. Brandeis Reappraised', *American Scholar*, vol. 54, no. 4, 1985; Urofsky, *Louis D. Brandeis: A Life*.

69 Alan T. Peacock and Hans Willgerodt (eds.), *Germany's Social Market Economy: Origins and Evolution*, New York, Palgrave Macmillan, 1989.

70 Franz Böhm, 'Kartellauflösung und Konzernentflechtung Spezialistenaufgabe uber Schicksalsfrage?', *Süddeutsche Juristen-Zeitung*, vol. 2, no. 9, 1947, pp. 504–5.

71 John Files, 'Lee Loevinger, 91, Kennedy-Era Antitrust Chief', *New York Times*, 8 May 2004.

72 Ibid.

73 Ben Brady, 'United States v. Alcoa and the Spread of American Law', (PhD diss., New York University, 2015), p. 29.

74 *United States v. Aluminum Co. of Am.*, 148 F.2d 416 (2d Cir. 1945).

75 Ibid.

76 Senator Kefauver, speaking on the Clayton Act, on 12 December 1950, 81st Cong., 2nd sess., *Congressional Record* 96, pt.12:16452.

77 'HR 2374. Amend an Act Entitled "An Act to Supplement Existing Laws Against Unlawful Restraints and Monopolies"', GovTrack, https://www.govtrack.us/congress/votes/81-1949/h94, (accessed 21 November 2019); 'HR 2374. Amend an Act Entitled "An Act to Supplement Existing Laws Against Unlawful Restraints and Monopolies"', GovTrack, https://www.govtrack.us/congress/votes/81-1950/s45, (accessed 21 November 2019).

78 U.S. Congress, Senate, *Hearings Before the Subcommittee of the Committee on Appropriations*, 80th Cong., 1st sess., 19 July 1948.

79 'The British Monopolies Act of 1948: A Contrast with American Policy and Practice', *Yale Law Journal*, vol. 59, no. 5, 1950, p. 899.

80 Serge Audier, 'A German Approach to Liberalism? Ordoliberalism, Sociological Liberalism, and Social Market Economy', *L'Economie Politique* 60, 2013–14, p. 48.

81 Steven H. Thal, 'The Existence of the Rule of Reason in the German Law against Trade Restraints: A Case Study Analysis', *New York University Journal of International Law and Politics*, vol. 3, no. 2, Winter 1970, p. 278.

82 Gregory Gethard, 'The German Economic Miracle', Investopedia [website], 17 September 2014, https://www.investopedia.com/articles/economics/09/german-economic-miracle.asp, (accessed 15 January 2020).

83 'Just Like Old Times', *Time*, 20 August 1963.

84 Quoted in Michael Schaller, *The American Occupation of Japan: Origins of the Cold War in Asia*, New York, Oxford University Press, 1985.

85 Ibid.

86 Kozo Yamamura, *Economic Policy in Postwar Japan: Growth Versus Economic Democracy*, Berkeley and Los Angeles, University of California Press, 1967.

87 Alissa A. Meade, 'Modeling a European Competition Authority', *Duke Law Journal* 46, 1996, p. 161.

88 'Trade Bloc Voids Deal by Grundig; French Distribution Accord Held Violation of Common Market Antitrust Policy', *New York Times*, 25 September 1964.

89 U.S. Congress, House of Representatives, Judiciary Committee, *Hearing Before Subcommittee No. 3*, 84th Cong., 1st sess., 9 March 1955, p. 31.

90 Capers Jones, *The Technical and Social History of Software Engineering*, New York, Addison-Wesley, 2014.

91 Susan P. Crawford, 'The Internet and the Project of Communications Law', *UCLA Law Review* 55 (2007); Barak D. Richman and Steven W. Usselman, 'Elhauge on Tying: Vindicated by History', *Tulsa Law Review*, 2014.

92 'Sandia and Its Management Contractor', Sandia National Laboratories, last modified 6 August 1997, https://www.sandia.gov/media/facts11.htm, (accessed 26 December 2019).

93 Gary E. Weir, 'The DEW Line – Cold War Defense at the Top of the World', Medium, last modified 12 March 2018, https://medium.com/@NGA_GEOINT/the-dew-line-cold-war-defense-at-the-top-of-the-world-fbafdd90a542, (accessed 26 December 2019).

94 James W. Cortada, *The Digital Flood: The Diffusion of Information Technology Across the U.S., Europe, and Asia*, New York, Oxford University Press, 2012; William D. Smith, 'I.B.M. Starts Early-Retirement Plan', *New York Times*, 31 August 1971.

95 Kevin Maney, *The Maverick and His Machine: Thomas Watson, Sr. and the Making of IBM*, Hoboken, Wiley, 2003.

96 United States Memorandum on the 1969 Case at 2, United States v. IBM, No. 72–344 (S.D.N.Y., 5 October 1995).

97 Stephen Brill, 'What to Tell Your Friends About IBM', *American Lawyer*, April 1982, p. 1.

98 William E. Kovacic, 'Designing Antitrust Remedies for Dominant Firm Misconduct', *Connecticut Law Review* 31, 1999, p. 1290.

99 Casey Leins, 'These States Benefit Most from the Software Industry', *U.S. News & World Report*, 19 September 2019, https://www.usnews.com/news/best-states/articles/2019-09-19/these-states-benefit-most-from-the-nations-software-industry, (accessed 27 December 2019).

NOTES

100 Robert W. Gomulkiewicz and Mary L. Williamson, 'A Brief Defense of Mass Market Software Agreements', *Rutgers Computer and Technology Law Journal* 22, 1996.

101 Jay Dratler, Jr., 'Microsoft as an Antitrust Target: IBM in Software?', *Southwestern Law Review* 25, 1996.

102 Stanley Gibson, 'Software Industry Born with IBM's Unbundling', *Computerworld*, 19 June 1989.

103 W. Edward Steinmuller, 'The U.S. Software Industry: An Analysis and Interpretive History', in David C. Mowery (ed.), *The International Computer Software Industry: A Comparative Study of Industry Evolution and Structure*, New York, Oxford University Press, 1995.

104 Frederick Betz, *Managing Technological Innovation: Competitive Advantage from Change*, 2nd ed., Hoboken, Wiley, 2003.

105 Jim Forbes, 'IBM Personal Computer', Selectric Typewriter Museum [website], http://selectric.org/archive/IBMPC2002/ibmpc.html, (accessed 27 December 2019).

106 Joseph F. Porac, 'Local Rationality, Global Blunders, and the Boundaries of Technological Choice: Lessons from IBM and DOS', in Raghu Garud et al. (eds.), *Technological Innovation: Oversights and Foresights*, New York, Cambridge University Press, 1997, p. 137.

107 Charles H. Ferguson and Charles R. Morris, *Computer Wars: The Post-IBM World*, Washington, Beard Books, 2003, pp. 26, 71.

108 *The Industrial Reorganization Act, Hearings Before the Subcommittee on Antitrust and Monopoly of the Committee on the Judiciary*, 93d Cong. 3840 (1974) (statement of Clay T. Whitehead, Director, Office of Telecommunications Policy, Executive Office of the President, accompanied by John Eger, Deputy Director).

109 Theodore N. Vail, 'Public Utilities and Public Policy', *Atlantic Monthly* 111, March 1913, p. 309.

110 In re. Use of the Carterfone Device, 13 F.C.C.2d 420 (1968).

111 Steve Coll, *The Deal of the Century: The Breakup of AT&T*, New York, Open Road Media, 2017.

112 Howard A. Shelanski, 'Adjusting Regulation to Competition: Toward a New Model for U.S. Telecommunications Policy', *Yale Journal on Regulation* 24, 2007.

113 Edward Feigenbaum and Pamela McCorduck, 'The Fifth Generation: Japan's Computing Challenge to the World', *Creative Computing*, vol. 10, no. 8, August 1984.

114 Joel West, 'Utopianism and National Competitiveness in Technology Rhetoric: The Case of Japan's Information Infrastructure', *Information Society*, vol. 12, no. 3, 1996, p. 256.

115 Andrew H. Thorson and Frank Siegfanz, 'The 1997 Deregulation of Japan's Holding Companies', *Pacific Rim Law and Policy Journal* 8, 1999.

116 Jonathan C. Comer and Thomas A. Wikle, 'Worldwide Diffusion of the Cellular Telephone, 1995–2005', *Professional Geographer* 60, 2011.

117 Bill Gates, 'The Internet Tidal Wave', Letters of Note, last modified 22 July 2011, http://www.lettersofnote.com/2011/07/internet-tidal-wave.html, (accessed 28 December 2019).

118 Microsoft originally licensed 86-DOS for $25,000, and later bought it for $50,000. Paul E. Ceruzzi, *A History of Modern Computing*, Cambridge, MIT Press, 2003.

119 *United States v. Microsoft Corp.*, 253 F3d 34 (D.C. Cir., 2001).

120 David Segal, 'Joel Klein, Hanging Tough', *Washington Post*, 24 March 1998.

121 Ellen Frankel Paul, 'Hayek on Monopoly and Antitrust in the Crucible of *United States v. Microsoft*', *NYU Journal of Law & Liberty*, vol. 1, no. 0, 2005, p. 174.

122 Douglas Martin, 'Aaron Director, Economist, Dies at 102', *New York Times*, 16 September 2004.

123 Donald Dewey, *The Antitrust Experiment in America*, New York, Columbia University Press, 1990, p. 25.

124 George Stigler, 'The Case Against Big Business', *Fortune*, May 1952.

125 Richard Posner, 'The Chicago School of Antitrust Analysis', in *The Making of Competition Policy: Legan and Economic Sources*, New York, Oxford University Press, 2013.

126 David Savage, 'Skeptical of Government Action: Bork Takes Narrow View on Antitrust Legislation', *Los Angeles Times*, 26 August 1987.

127 Martin, 'Director'.

128 Edmund Kitch, 'The Fire of Truth: A Remembrance of Law and Economics at Chicago, 1932–1970', *Journal of Law and Economics*, vol. 26, no. 1, April 1983, p. 183.

129 John McGee, 'Commentary', in Harvey Goldschmid, Harold Mann, John Weston (eds.), *Industrial Concentration: The New Learning*, Boston, Little, Brown, 1974, p. 104.

130 Green Paper on Vertical Restraints. See Commission (EU), 'Green Paper on Vertical Restraints in EC Competition Policy' (Green Paper on Vertical Restraints) COM (96) 721 final, 22 January 1997, p. 17.

131 Neelie Kroes, Member of the European Commission, 'European Competition Policy – Delivering Better Markets and Better Choices' (speech, London, 15 September 2005), European Commission, ec.europa.eu/commission/presscorner/detail/en/SPEECH_05_512, (accessed 28 December 2019).

132 Anthony Giorgianni, 'How to Avoid Being Gouged When Buying Eyeglasses', *Consumer Reports*, 29 December 2016; David Lazarus, 'Column: How Badly Are We Being Ripped Off on Eyewear? Former Industry Exec Tells All', *Los Angeles Times*, 5 March 2019.

133 'Vogue Eyewear', Luxottica, http://www.luxottica.com/en/eyewear-brands/vogue-eyewear, (accessed 18 November 2019).

134 Valentina Za and Sudip Kar-Gupta, 'Luxottica and Essilor in 46 Billion Euro Merger to Create Eyewear Giant', Reuters, 15 January 2017.

135 'Sticker Shock: Why Are Glasses So Expensive?', *60 Minutes*, 7 October 2012.

136 'Justice Department Requires Anheuser-Busch InBev to Divest Stake in MillerCoors and Alter Beer Distributor Practices as Part of SABMiller Acquisition', Department of Justice, 20 July 2016.

137 Peter Hayes, *Industry and Ideology: IG Farben in the Nazi Era*, Cambridge, Cambridge University Press, 1987, p. xii.

138 Camila Domonoske, 'Monsanto No More: Agri-Chemical Giant's Name Dropped in Bayer Acquisition', NPR, 4 June 2018.

139 'DowDuPont Merger Successfully Completed', Dow Corporate, 1 September 2017.

140 Reuters, 'ChemChina Clinches Its $43 Billion Takeover of Syngenta', *Fortune*, 5 May 2017.

141 'High Drug Prices & Monopoly', Open Markets Institute, https://openmarketsinstitute.org/explainer/high-drug-prices-and-monopoly/, (accessed 18 November 2019).

142 Katy Milani, and Devin Duffy, 'Profit Over Patients: How the Rules of our Economy Encourage the Pharmaceutical Industry's Extractive Behavior', Roosevelt Institute, February 2019, p. 4.

143 Barack Obama (speech, Oregon, 18 May 2008), Reuters.

144 Adam Satariano, 'Europe's Margrethe Vestager Takes a Rare Step Toward Big Tech', *New York Times*, 16 October 2019.

145 John Perry Barlow, 'Electronic Frontier: Coming Into The Country', *Communications of the ACM*, vol. 34, no. 3, March 1991, p. 19.

146 Nicholas Carlson, 'Here's The Biggest Threat To Facebook, And What Facebook Is Doing About It', *Business Insider*, 6 February 2012.

147 Victor Luckerson, 'Here's Proof That Instagram Was One Of The Smartest Acquisitions Ever', *Time*, 19 April 2016.

148 United Kingdom, Office of Fair Trading, *Anticipated Acquisition by Facebook Inc of Instagram Inc*, Case ME/5525/12, 14 August 2012.

149 Parmy Olson, 'Facebook Closes $19 Billion WhatsApp Deal', *Forbes*, 6 October 2014.

150 Paige Cooper, 'Social Media Advertising Stats That Matter to Marketers in 2018', Hootsuite, 5 June 2018, https://blog.hootsuite.com/social-media-advertising-stats/, (accessed 1 January 2020).

151 Tim Wu and Stuart A. Thompson, 'The Roots of Big Tech Run Disturbingly Deep', *New York Times*, 7 June 2019.

152 Josh Constine, 'A Year Later, $19 Billion For WhatsApp Doesn't Sound So Crazy', TechCrunch, 19 February 2015.

153 'Facebook's WhatsApp Acquisition Exposes Grave Risks To The Business Model', SeekingAlpha [website], 20 February 2014, https://seekingalpha.com/article/2034463-facebooks-whatsapp-acquisition-exposes-grave-risks-to-the-business-model, (accessed 15 January 2020).

154 The US Government, in the course of an investigation, told Google to knock it off, and Google grudgingly stopped taking Yelp's reviews, though it insisted it was doing Yelp a favour.

155 Peter Thiel, 'Competition Is for Losers', *Wall Street Journal*, 12 September 2014.

156 'Company Info', Facebook, https://about.fb.com/company-info/, (accessed 15 January 2020).

157 Rani Molla, 'Mary Meeker: China now has nine of the world's biggest internet companies – almost as many as the U.S.', *Vox*, 30 May 2018.

158 'To Cover China, There's No Substitute for WeChat', *New York Times*, 9 January 2019.

159 Gregory Allen, 'Understanding China's AI Strategy', Center for New American Security, 6 February 2019, https://www.cnas.org/publications/reports/understanding-chinas-ai-strategy, (accessed 1 January 2020).

160 Eva Dou, 'Jailed for a Text: China's Censors Are Spying on Mobile Chat Groups', *Wall Street Journal*, 8 December 2017.

NOTES

161 'How Private Are Your Favourite Messaging Apps?', Amnesty
    International, 21 October 2016, https://www.amnesty.org/en/latest/
    campaigns/2016/10/which-messaging-apps-best-protect-your-privacy/,
    (accessed 1 January 2020).

162 Shannon Bond, 'Mark Zuckerberg Offers A Choice: The Facebook
    Way Or The China Way', NPR, 23 October 2019.

163 *Brown Shoe Co. v. United States*, 370 U.S. 294 (1962).

164 European Commission, 'Council Regulation (EC) No 139/2004 of 20
    January 2004 on the control of concentrations between undertakings
    (the EC Merger Regulation)', *Official Journal of the European Union* 47,
    L 24, 29 January 2004.

165 Tripp Mickle and Brent Kendall, 'Justice Department Clears AB
    InBev's Takeover of SABMiller', *Wall Street Journal*, 20 July 2016.

166 Jack Ewing, 'E.U. Blocks Siemens-Alstom Plan to Create European
    Train Giant', *New York Times*, 6 February 2019.

167 Julia Werdigier and Matthew Saltmarsh, 'Report Suggests Breakup of
    British Airport Operator', *New York Times*, 21 August 2008.

168 Gunnar Niels, Helen Jenkins and James Kavanagh, *Economics for
    Competition Lawyers*, Oxford, Oxford University Press, 2011, p. 471.

169 *Chicago Board of Trade v. United States*, 246 U.S. 231 (1918).

170 Andrew Davis, 'Why Amazon Paid No 2018 Federal Income Tax',
    CNBC.com, 4 April 2019, https://www.cnbc.com/2019/04/03/why-
    amazon-paid-no-federal-income-tax.html, (accessed 1 January 2020).

INDEX

INDEX

INDEX

INDEX